teach yourself
QUICK-METHOD QUILTING

*G*uided by our new book, Teach Yourself Quick-Method Quilting, *even beginners can learn the speediest and most accurate ways to cut and piece quilts. Our step-by-step directions and color diagrams lead you through the ABC's of today's faster and easier quilting methods — from how to select the right tools and fabrics to the best approaches for quilting it all together. This handy primer includes a variety of projects, such as patchwork pillows and wall hangings, that let you put your new, up-to-date skills into practice. Not only will this guide help you master the patterns inside, but it will also be an indispensable reference that you'll turn to again and again. So let the quilting class begin, and before you know it, you'll be piecing your favorite blocks the quick-method way!*

LEISURE ARTS, INC.
Little Rock, Arkansas

D1362032

EDITORIAL STAFF

Vice President and Editor-in-Chief:
  Anne Van Wagner Childs
Executive Director: Sandra Graham Case
Editorial Director: Susan Frantz Wiles
Publications Director: Carla Bentley
Creative Art Director: Gloria Bearden
Senior Graphics Art Director: Melinda Stout

DESIGN
Design Director:
  Patricia Wallenfang Sowers
Senior Designer: Linda Diehl Tiano

PRODUCTION
Managing Editor: Sherry Taylor O'Connor
Senior Technical Writer:
  Kathleen Coughran Magee
Technical Writer:
  Barbara McClintock Vechik

EDITORIAL
Managing Editor: Linda L. Trimble
Associate Editor: Terri Leming Davidson
Assistant Editors:
  Tammi Williamson Bradley,
  Robyn Sheffield-Edwards, and
  Darla Burdette Kelsay
Copy Editor: Laura Lee Weland

ART
Graphics Art Director:
  Rhonda Hodge Shelby
Senior Graphics Illustrator: Dana Vaughn
Graphics Illustrators: Sonya McFatrich,
  Brent Miller, Katie Murphy, Mary Ellen
  Wilhelm, and Dianna K. Winters
Photography Stylists: Christina Tiano Myers,
  Karen Smart Hall, and Aurora Huston

BUSINESS STAFF

Publisher: Bruce Akin
Vice President, Finance: Tom Siebenmorgen
Vice President, Retail Sales:
  Thomas L. Carlisle
Retail Sales Director: Richard Tignor
Vice President, Retail Marketing:
  Pam Stebbins
Retail Marketing Director:
  Margaret Sweetin
Retail Customer Services Manager:
  Carolyn Pruss
General Merchandise Manager: Russ Barnett
Distribution Director: Ed M. Strackbein
Vice President, Marketing: Guy A. Crossley
Marketing Manager: Byron L. Taylor
Print Production Manager: Laura Lockhart
Print Production Coordinator:
  Nancy Reddick Baker

Library of Congress Catalog Number 96-77060
International Standard Book Number 1-57486-057-7

TABLE OF CONTENTS

QUICK-METHOD ABC'S

PRACTICE MAKES PERFECT

QUICK-METHOD ABC'S

This handy primer has everything you need to teach yourself the latest rotary cutting and speed-piecing techniques. We've also included basic finishing information to help you complete your projects. You can turn to this comprehensive reference guide for all your quiltmaking questions!

QUILTING
SUPPLIES

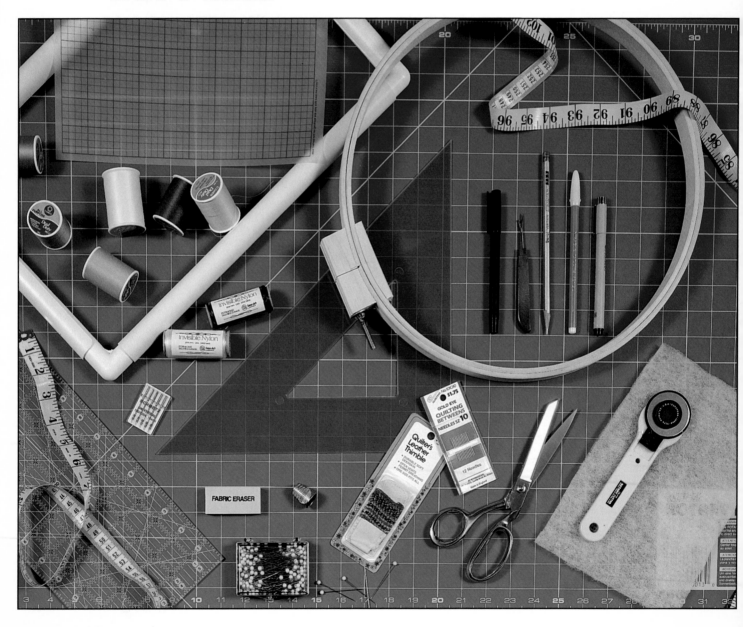

This list includes all the tools and supplies you'll need for basic quick-method quiltmaking. Almost all of these items can be found at your local quilt shop or fabric store. Many brands of tools are available, so choosing one brand over another may seem like an overwhelming task. Talking to other quilters and fabric store or quilt shop owners is one of the best ways to find out which brands work well.

CUTTING SUPPLIES

Rotary cutter — One of the easiest ways to describe a rotary cutter is to say that it looks like a pizza cutter. The cutter consists of a round, sharp blade mounted on a handle. There are several sizes available. We recommend the cutter with the 45mm or 1³/₄" diameter blade. Look for a rotary cutter with a manual retractable blade guard for safety. If you are left-handed, make sure the rotary cutter is adaptable for left-handed use.

Rotary cutting blades — It is always helpful to have a spare blade on hand for your cutter. Blades will last a long time, but when your blade begins to skip threads or will not cut fabric easily, change blades or use one of the rotary cutting blade sharpeners that are available. If you decide to discard your blade, carefully wrap the blade in paper before you throw it away. Blades that are dull for fabric are still sharp and dangerous.

Rotary cutting rulers — A rotary cutting ruler is a thick, clear ruler made specifically for use with a rotary cutter. It should have accurate ¹/₈" crosswise and lengthwise markings and markings for 30°, 45°, and 60° angles. A 6" x 24" ruler is a good size for most cutting — it's long enough to cut 45"w fabric when the fabric is folded in half. If you need to make a cut that is wider than your ruler, you will need an additional ruler, such as a 6", 12¹/₂", or 15" square ruler.

Cutting mat — This special mat is designed to be used with a rotary cutter. An 18" x 24" (or larger) mat is a good size for most cutting. Commonly used 45"w fabrics will easily fit on a 24"w mat when fabrics are folded in half. Look for a mat that is "self healing." When a cut is made on the mat, the cut seems to almost disappear, and the mat is not nicked. The surface of the mat should also provide enough friction to keep the fabric from sliding. Store your mat flat and away from heat and direct sunlight.

Triangle — A large plastic right-angle triangle (available in art and office supply stores) is useful in rotary cutting for making first cuts to "square up" raw edges of fabric and for checking to see that cuts remain at right angles to the fold.

Paper — Tracing paper is needed for tracing patterns and making trimming templates. Drafting paper with 8 squares to the inch is helpful when drafting shapes for rotary cutting.

PIECING SUPPLIES

Sewing machine — A sewing machine that produces a good, even straight stitch is all that is necessary for most piecing. Use size 10 to 14 or 70 to 90 universal needles for woven fabrics in your machine. Clean and oil your machine as directed and keep the tension set properly.

Iron — An iron with both steam and dry settings and a smooth, clean soleplate is necessary for proper pressing.

Pins — Straight pins made especially for quilting are extra long with large, round heads. Glass head and plastic head pins are available. Some quilters prefer extra-fine dressmaker's silk pins. Pins should be sharp and clean so that they will slide easily in and out of the fabric.

Sewing thread — General-purpose sewing thread is used for basting and piecing. Buy high-quality cotton or cotton-covered polyester thread in light and dark neutrals, such as ecru and grey, for your basic supplies.

Scissors — A sharp pair of fabric scissors may be used for trimming "dog ears" on pieces. A separate pair of scissors for cutting paper and plastic is recommended. You may also wish to keep a small pair of scissors handy for clipping threads.

Seam ripper — A good seam ripper with a fine point is useful for removing stitches.

Masking Tape — Masking tape can be used to make a ¹/₄" stitching guide for your sewing machine. Two widths of masking tape, 1"w and ¹/₄"w, are also helpful when quilting. The ¹/₄"w tape may be used as a guide when outline quilting. The 1"w tape is used to secure the backing fabric to a flat surface when layering a quilt.

Tape measure — A flexible 120" long tape measure is helpful for measuring a quilt top before adding borders.

FINISHING SUPPLIES

Batting — Used for the middle layer of a quilt, batting is most commonly available in polyester, cotton, or a cotton/polyester blend (see **Choosing and Preparing the Batting**, pg. 33).

Quilting hoop or frame — Specialty hoops or frames are designed to securely hold the 3 layers of a quilt together while you quilt. Many different types and sizes are available, including round and oval wooden hoops, frames made of rigid plastic pipe, and large floor frames made of either material. A 14" or 16" hoop allows you to quilt in your lap and makes your quilting portable. An embroidery hoop should not be considered a substitute for a quilting hoop, since the bands of an embroidery hoop are not wide enough to securely hold multiple layers.

Needles — Two types of needles are used for hand sewing: betweens and sharps. Used for hand quilting, *betweens* are short needles that come in numbered sizes such as 8, 10, and 12. Betweens are shorter than regular sewing needles and allow you to work through layered fabric and make small stitches. You may wish to begin with a size 8. In order to achieve smaller stitches, try a size 10 or 12. *Sharps* are longer needles used for basting and other hand sewing. For hand sewing needles, the higher the number, the smaller the needle.

Quilting thread — Quilting thread is stronger than general-purpose sewing thread, and some brands have a coating to make them slide more easily through the quilt layers. Although most quilting is done with ecru or white thread, the color of quilting thread used is simply a matter of personal choice.

Thimble — A thimble is necessary when hand quilting. Thimbles are available in metal, plastic, and leather and come in many sizes. Using a thimble may seem awkward at first, but soon you'll find you won't want to work without one. Choose a thimble that fits well and is comfortable.

Needle threader — A needle threader helps to thread a needle with a small eye, such as a between.

Marking tools — There are many different types of marking tools available for fabric (see **Marking Quilting Lines**, pg. 32).

Eraser — A soft white fabric eraser or white art eraser may be used to remove some pencil marks from fabric. Do not use a colored eraser, as the dye may discolor fabric.

Template material — Sheets of translucent plastic, often pre-marked with a grid, are made especially for making templates and quilting stencils. Lightweight cardboard, such as poster board and legal-size manila folders, may be used to make some quilting templates.

Permanent fine-point marker — A marker is used to mark quilting templates and stencils and to sign and date your quilts. Test marker on fabric to make sure it will not bleed on fabric or wash out.

FABRICS

SELECTING FABRICS

For many quilters, choosing fabrics for a new quilt project is one of the most fun, yet most challenging, parts of quiltmaking. The colors in your quilt are seen first, even before design and workmanship.

Photographs of quilts are excellent guides for choosing the colors for your quilt. You may choose to duplicate the colors in the photograph, or you may use the same light, medium, and dark values in completely different color families. For example, you may wish to change the **Shoofly Lap Quilt,** pg. 44, from shades of tan to shades of blue.

Your fabrics should have contrast — dark and light, large prints and small prints, prints and solids. This will make your quilt more exciting to the eye.

The most important thing to remember when selecting your fabrics is to choose fabrics you like. There are many beautiful quilts that use fabric and color combinations you would never think to use. If you like your choices, go ahead and get started with the assurance that you will like the finished product.

For quilting, choose high-quality, closely woven 100% cotton fabrics. All-cotton fabrics hold a crease better, fray less, and are easier to quilt than cotton/polyester blends. All the fabrics for a quilt should be of comparable weight and weave. Check the ends of the fabric bolts for fabric content and width.

The yardage requirements listed for each project are based on 45"w fabric with a "usable" width of 40" after shrinkage and trimming selvages. Your actual usable width will probably vary from fabric to fabric. Most fabrics will yield 40" or more, but if you find a fabric that yields a narrower width, you will need to purchase additional yardage to compensate. The recommended yardage lengths should be adequate for occasional resquaring of fabric when many cuts are required. However, it never hurts to buy a little more fabric for insurance against a narrower usable width, the occasional cutting error, or to have on hand for making other quilts or coordinating projects.

You will also need about 1 yard of fabric to practice cutting techniques, to familiarize yourself with your cutter, ruler, and mat, and to perform a sewing test.

A Note About Directional Fabrics

There are many beautiful directional fabrics on the market today. These are fabrics such as plaids, stripes, and fabrics with designs printed in obvious rows. They require special attention when purchasing, cutting, and sewing. Directional fabrics can add dimension and personality to a quilt, but you must choose them with care and treat them differently from solid or non-directional fabrics.

The designs on some directional fabrics are not printed straight on the fabric, making it very difficult to rotary cut large pieces and keep the designs straight. Before you purchase a directional fabric, unfold it and check to make sure the design is printed straight on the fabric. You will also want to purchase an additional 1/2 to 1 yard. The extra fabric will enable you to line up your ruler with the design of the fabric if it is printed off grain, rather than following the straight grain of the fabric.

Although you usually cut pieces following the grain line of the fabric, if you want the design of a directional fabric to be straight in your cut pieces, the design of the fabric will override the grain line. You will need to cut one layer at a time instead of folding the fabric as in most rotary cutting. If the fabric is folded, you will not be able to see the design underneath.

You will also need to pay special attention when sewing together pieces that may be cut slightly off grain, as you may be working with bias edges which stretch easily.

PREPARING FABRICS

All fabrics should be washed, dried, and pressed before you begin work on your quilt. Even if you do not plan to wash your quilt in the future, you should wash the fabric to remove sizing, pre-shrink the fabric, and check for colorfastness. Washing also makes the fabric easier to quilt and will remove excess dyes and chemicals that may shorten the life of your quilt.

1. Dark colors such as red, blue, or black may bleed when washed. To check colorfastness before washing, fill a sink about half full with hot water and add a little mild laundry detergent. Place one end of fabric in the water and swish it around. Squeeze water from fabric into a clear glass. If water is not clear, machine wash fabric separately until rinse water runs clear. Some fabrics just contain excess dyes and will stop bleeding after one or two washings. Others will continue to bleed. If the fabric continues to bleed, choose another fabric, or a red and white quilt may become a red and pink quilt.

2. To wash fabrics, unfold yardage and separate fabrics by color. To help reduce raveling, use scissors to snip a small triangle from each corner of your fabric (**Fig. 1**). Machine wash fabrics in warm water using mild laundry detergent or soap made for quilts and fine fabrics. Do not use fabric softener. Rinse well to make sure all chemicals are removed from fabric. Dry fabric in the dryer, checking long fabric lengths occasionally to make sure that they are not tangling.

Fig. 1

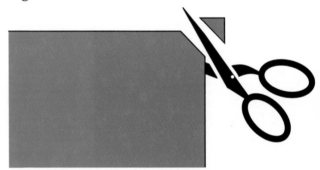

3. To make ironing easier, remove fabrics from the dryer while they are slightly damp. Press each fabric with iron set on "cotton."

7

ROTARY CUTTING

Rotary cutting has grown in popularity in recent years. Two of the major reasons are speed and accuracy. You save time because you don't have to trace around templates and cut out each piece individually with scissors. And your cut pieces are generally more accurate because you're checking them against a ruler with every cut you make!

In the rotary cutting process, strips are cut first, then shapes such as squares, rectangles, triangles, and diamonds are cut from the strips. Multiple layers of fabric can be cut simultaneously, saving even more time.

Pieces are cut with ¼" seam allowances included. There is only an occasional need to mark your seam allowance or make templates.

SAFETY FIRST

Observe safety precautions when using the rotary cutter, since it is extremely sharp. Develop good safety habits from the very beginning and practice those habits faithfully.

- Always keep your rotary cutter away from children.
- Retract the blade guard just before making a cut and close it immediately afterward, before laying down the cutter. This will add only seconds of time, but may save you or someone else from an injury.
- Always cut in a direction away from your body.
- When working on a large project, take breaks when you need them. Your shoulder and wrist may become tired, causing you to be more prone to an accident.

CUTTING CROSSWISE STRIPS

Most pieces for a quilt top are cut from strips that are cut from the selvage-to-selvage width (crosswise grain) of the fabric. Therefore, becoming comfortable with cutting crosswise strips is one of the cornerstones of effective rotary cutting.

1. Fold a length of washed, dried, and pressed fabric lengthwise (as it was on the bolt) with right sides out and matching selvages. If necessary, adjust slightly at selvages so that the fold lies flat.

2. Place your cutting mat on a clean, flat surface that is at a comfortable height. Place fabric on the cutting mat with the fold of the fabric close to you and the fabric extending to your right.

3. To straighten the uneven fabric edge and "square up" the fabric, place a right angle triangle on the fabric about 1" from the left raw edge with the lower edge of the triangle carefully aligned with the fold. Place the right edge of the rotary cutting ruler over the left raw edge of the fabric and against the triangle (**Fig. 2**).

Fig. 2

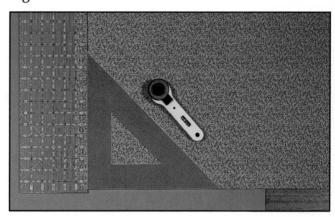

4. Hold the ruler firmly in place with your left hand, making sure to anchor your pinkie finger on the cutting mat (**Fig. 3**). Remove the triangle, pick up the rotary cutter, and retract the blade guard. Place the blade of the rotary cutter directly against the right edge of the ruler. Using a firm, even motion, begin rolling the cutter before the fold and continue cutting until the rotary cutter is about even with your fingers. At this point, use an "inchworm" motion to move your thumb close to your fingers (**Fig. 4**) and then move your fingers ahead 5" or 6", always keeping pressure on the ruler. Roll the cutter even with fingers again. Continue cutting and "inching" until you have cut the entire width of fabric. Close the blade guard. The edge of your fabric is now squared up. (**Note:** If you try holding the ruler at the end or in the middle without moving your hand, the ruler is likely to slip.)

Fig. 3

Fig. 4

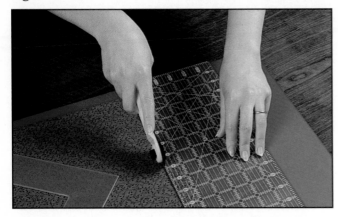

5. After squaring up, cut the strips required for the project. Place the ruler over the cut edge of the fabric, aligning the desired marking on the ruler with the cut edge. For example, if instructions call for a 3" strip, align the 3" marking on the ruler with the cut edge of the fabric (**Fig. 5**).

Fig. 5

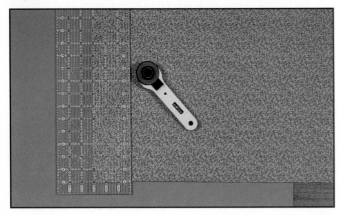

6. When cutting several strips from a single piece of fabric, it is important to occasionally use the ruler and triangle to ensure the cuts are still at a perfect right angle to the fold. If not, repeat Steps 3 and 4 to square up the cut edge. If a cut is not made at a right angle to the fold, the strip will not be straight. It will be slightly bent or have a "V" shape (**Fig. 6**).

Fig. 6

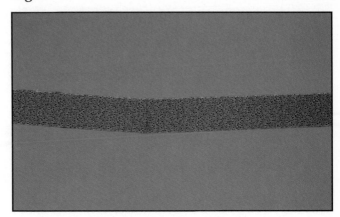

7. Before you cut shapes from a strip, you must square up the strip ends to establish a right angle. To square up selvage ends of a strip, refer to **Fig. 7** and place folded strip on mat with selvage ends to your right. Aligning a horizontal marking on ruler with 1 long edge of strip, use rotary cutter to trim off selvage to make end of strip square and even (**Fig. 7**).

Fig. 7

8. Turn strip (or entire mat) so that the cut end is to your left before making subsequent cuts. There are times when it is easier to turn the cutting mat or walk around the cutting surface to work at the correct angle instead of moving the fabric pieces. If you must move a stack of pieces, make sure the pieces do not shift. You may have to cut the pieces individually if they shift.

9. Pieces such as squares and rectangles can now be cut from strips. (When cutting shapes such as diamonds, equilateral triangles, and parallelograms, the selvages will be removed at the same time a correct angle is established for cutting.) Usually strips remain folded and pieces are cut in pairs after selvages are removed. There may be times when you have to open the fold to cut 1 last piece from a strip.

10. After some practice, you may want to try stacking up to 6 fabric layers when making cuts. When stacking strips, match long cut edges and follow Step 7 to square up ends of strip stack. Carefully turn stack (or entire mat) so that squared-up ends are to your left before making subsequent cuts. After cutting, check accuracy of pieces. Some shapes, such as diamonds, are more difficult to cut accurately in stacks.

CUTTING STRIPS WIDER THAN YOUR RULER

When cutting a strip that is wider than your ruler, you can place 2 rulers side by side to achieve the measurement. For example, if you wish to cut a 9"w strip and you are working with a 6"w ruler, first square up the fabric. Next, place your second ruler on the fabric with the 3" markings aligned with the left edge of fabric. Place your 6"w ruler directly against it (**Fig. 8**). The 2 measurements add up to 9". Remove your extra ruler. Place your left hand firmly on your 6"w ruler and make the cut (**Fig. 9**).

Fig. 8

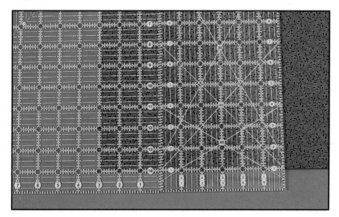

Fig. 9

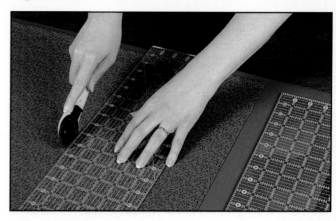

CUTTING STRIP SETS

In some cases, strips will be sewn together into strip sets before being cut into smaller units. When cutting a strip set, align a seam in the strip set with a horizontal marking on the ruler to maintain square cuts (**Fig. 10**). We do not recommend stacking strip sets for rotary cutting.

Fig. 10

CUTTING LENGTHWISE STRIPS

We recommend cutting most borders and long sashing strips along the more stable lengthwise grain of the fabric to minimize wavy edges caused by stretching and to eliminate piecing. When cutting borders or sashings that are shorter than the usable width of your fabric (about 40"), you can cut them along the crosswise grain, since the strips are not long enough to cause a problem with stretching.

There are 2 methods for cutting lengthwise strips. The first method will probably seem a little easier, the second one a little faster. Try both methods and use the one you are most comfortable with.

Method 1 for Cutting Lengthwise Strips

1. To remove selvages before cutting lengthwise strips, follow Steps 1 - 4 of **Cutting Crosswise Strips**, pg. 8, to square up one end of the fabric. Place fabric on mat with selvages to your left and squared-up end at bottom of mat. Placing ruler over selvage and using squared-up edge instead of fold, repeat Steps 3 and 4, pg. 8, to cut away selvages as you did raw edges (**Fig. 11**). After making a cut the length of the mat, move the next section of fabric to be cut onto the mat. Repeat until you have removed selvages from the required length of fabric.

Fig. 11

2. After removing selvages, place fabric with squared-up end at bottom of mat. Place ruler over left edge of fabric, aligning desired marking on ruler with cut edge of fabric; make cut.

Method 2 for Cutting Lengthwise Strips

1. Fold a length of washed, dried, and pressed fabric with wrong sides together and selvages at both ends of fabric. Make sure fabric is straight at the fold and carefully fold fabric over again (**Fig. 12**). Place fabric on mat with selvages on the left and right and folds at top and bottom.

Fig. 12

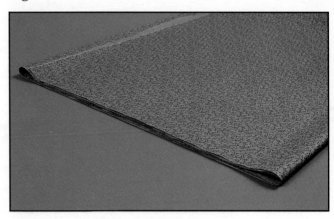

2. Follow Steps 3 and 4 of **Cutting Crosswise Strips**, pg. 8, to remove left selvage and square up fabric. If the entire length of fabric does not fit on the cutting mat, make a cut, then move the next section of fabric to be cut onto the mat.
3. After removing selvage, place ruler over left edge of fabric, aligning desired marking on ruler with cut edge of fabric, and make cut.

SHAPES

Now that you're familiar with cutting strips, you're ready to cut specific shapes from the strips. The following sections identify each shape, show you how to figure the size of the shape you need, then provide an example so you can follow along to see these numbers in action.

CUTTING SQUARES

What They Are: Squares are one of the most common shapes in quiltmaking. They have 4 sides which are equal in length. All angles are right (90°) angles.

Numbers You Need: To cut a square, add 1/2" to the finished height and 1/2" to the finished length.

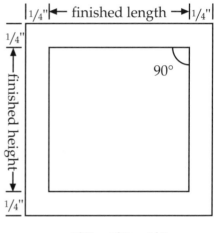

1/4" + 1/4" = 1/2"

Try It Out: Cut a 1½" finished square.

1. Cut your fabric strip 2"w *(1½" finished height + ½")*.
2. Square up selvage end of strip and place squared-up end to your left.
3. Place ruler on fabric with 2" marked line *(1½" finished length + ½")* aligned with cut edge of strip and make cut (**Fig. 13**).

Fig. 13

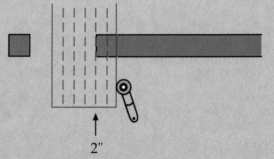

2"

4. You now have a 2" square. When sewn into a block, the square will finish 1½" x 1½".

What They Are: Rectangles have 4 sides with opposite sides equal in length. All angles are right (90°) angles.

Numbers You Need: To cut a rectangle, add ¹/₂" to the finished height and ¹/₂" to the finished length.

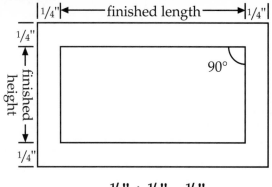

$$¼" + ¼" = ½"$$

Try It Out: Cut a 1" x 2" finished rectangle.

1. Cut your fabric strip 1¹/₂"w (*1" finished height + ¹/₂"*).
2. Square up selvage end of strip and place squared-up end to your left.
3. Place ruler on fabric with 2¹/₂" marked line (*2" finished length + ¹/₂"*) aligned with cut edge of strip and make cut (**Fig. 14**).

Fig. 14

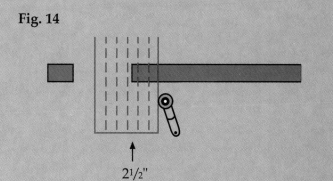

2¹/₂"

4. You now have a 1¹/₂" x 2¹/₂" rectangle. When sewn into a block, the rectangle will finish 1" x 2".

13

What They Are: As the name implies, half-square triangles are triangles made when a square is cut in half once diagonally. Each triangle has a right (90°) angle and 2 sides that are equal in length. Half-square triangles are cut when the short sides of the triangle will be on the outside of a block or unit. This will ensure that the short sides will be cut on the straight grain.

Numbers You Need: To cut this triangle, add 7/8" to the finished height and 7/8" to the finished length.

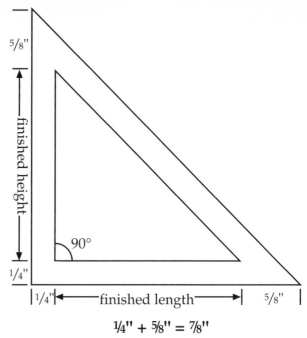

1/4" + 5/8" = 7/8"

Try It Out: Cut a 2" finished half-square triangle.

1. Cut your fabric strip 2⅞"w (*2" finished height + ⅞"*).
2. Square up selvage end of strip and place squared-up end to your left.
3. Place ruler on strip with 2⅞" marked line (*2" finished length + ⅞"*) aligned with left edge of strip and make cut (**Fig. 15**). You will have a square that measures 2⅞" x 2⅞".

Fig. 15

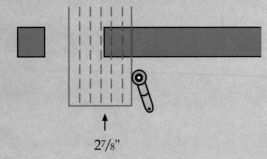

2⅞"

4. Place ruler diagonally on square with edge of ruler aligned with opposite corners and make cut (**Fig. 16**). Each square produces 2 triangles.

Fig. 16

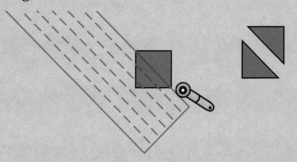

5. You now have two 2⅞" half-square triangles. When sewn into a block, each triangle will finish 2"h and 2"l. If you sew two 2⅞" half-square triangles together, you will make a square with a finished size of 2".

What They Are: Quarter-square triangles are triangles made when a square is cut twice diagonally into quarters. Each triangle has a right angle and 2 sides that are equal in length. Quarter-square triangles are cut so that the long side will be on the straight grain. Use them when the long side of the triangle will be on the outside of a unit or block.

Numbers You Need: To cut this triangle, add 1¹/₄" to the finished length of the long side.

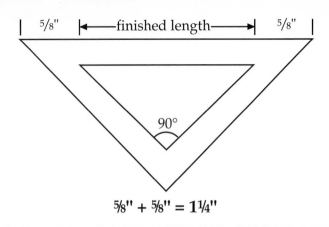

$$5\!/\!8" + 5\!/\!8" = 1\tfrac{1}{4}"$$

Try It Out: Cut a 2" finished quarter-square triangle.

1. Cut your fabric strip 3¹/₄"w *(2" finished length of long side + 1¹/₄ ")*.
2. Square up selvage end of strip and place squared-up end to your left.
3. Place ruler on strip with 3¹/₄" marked line *(2" finished length + 1¹/₄ ")* aligned with left edge of strip and make cut (**Fig. 17**). You will have a square that measures 3¹/₄" x 3¹/₄".

Fig. 17

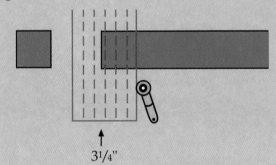

3¹/₄"

4. Place ruler diagonally on square with edge of ruler aligned with opposite corners and make cut (**Fig. 18**). Cut diagonally again (**Fig. 19**). Each square produces 4 triangles.

Fig. 18

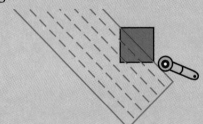

Fig. 19

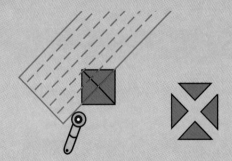

5. You now have four 3¹/₄" quarter-square triangles. When sewn into a block, each triangle will finish 2" on the long edge.

What They Are: Equilateral triangles are triangles with all 3 sides equal in length. All angles are 60°.

Numbers You Need: To cut this triangle, add ³/4" to the finished height.

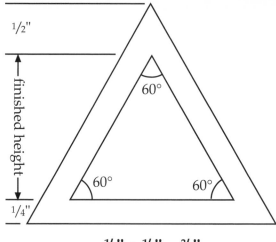

½" + ¼" = ¾"

Try It Out: Cut an equilateral triangle with a finished height of 1¹/2".

1. Cut your fabric strip 2¹/4"w (*1¹/2" finished height + ³/4"*).
2. Turn mat or strip so selvages are to your right.
3. Place ruler on strip with bottom 60° line on ruler aligned with bottom edge of strip and make cut (**Fig. 20**). This will remove the selvage and establish a 60° angle.

Fig. 20

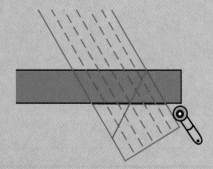

4. To cut a triangle, place ruler on fabric with top 60° line on ruler aligned with bottom edge of strip and edge of ruler even with top corner of strip and make cut (**Fig. 21**).

Fig. 21

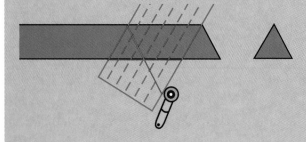

5. To cut a second triangle from the strip, place ruler on strip with bottom 60° line on ruler aligned with bottom edge of strip and edge of ruler even with bottom corner of strip and make cut (**Fig. 22**). You can alternate placing the top and bottom 60° line of the ruler along the bottom strip edge to cut as many triangles as you need.

Fig. 22

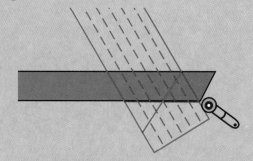

6. You now have 2 equilateral triangles that are 2¹/4"h. When sewn into a block, each triangle will finish 1¹/2"h.

What They Are: Diamonds have 2 pairs of parallel sides with opposite angles equal. All sides of a diamond are equal in length. Diamonds may have different angles, such as 30°, 45°, and 60° (measure the narrow angle).

To cut a diamond, you must know the angle (measure the narrow angle) and the finished height or width (they are the same).

Numbers You Need: To cut a diamond, add ½" to the finished height or width.

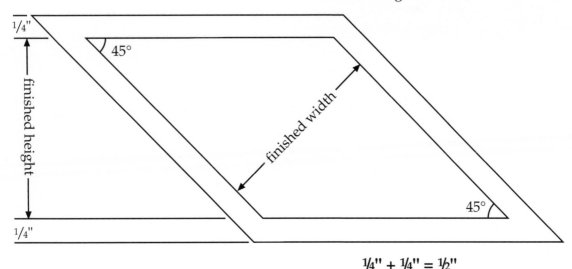

$$¼" + ¼" = ½"$$

Try It Out: Cut a 45° diamond with a finished height of 1⅞".

1. Cut your fabric strip 2⅜"w (*1⅞" finished height + ½"*).
2. Turn mat or strip so that selvages are to your right.
3. Place ruler on strip with 45° line on ruler aligned with bottom edge of strip (**Fig. 23**) and make cut. This will remove the selvage and establish a 45° angle.

Fig. 23

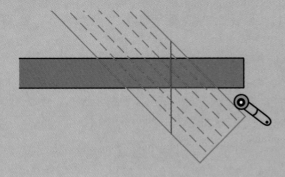

4. Turn strip or mat so 45° edge is to your left. Place ruler on strip with 45° line aligned with bottom edge of strip and 2⅜" line (*1⅞" finished width + ½"*) aligned with 45° edge; make cut (**Fig. 24**).

Fig. 24

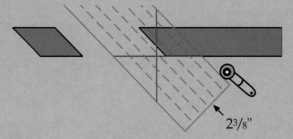

2⅜"

5. You now have a 45° diamond. When sewn into a block, the diamond will finish 1⅞"h and 1⅞"w.

What They Are: A parallelogram is an elongated diamond with opposite sides parallel and each pair of sides equal in length. In quilt blocks, a parallelogram will commonly have a narrow angle of 30°, 45°, or 60°.

To cut a parallelogram, you must know the angle (measure the narrow angle), the finished height, and the finished length.

Numbers You Need: To cut a parallelogram, add the following amounts to the finished height and length:

Angle of parallelogram	Amount to add to finished height	Amount to add to finished length
30° angle	1/2"	1"
45° angle	1/2"	3/4"
60° angle	1/2"	9/16"

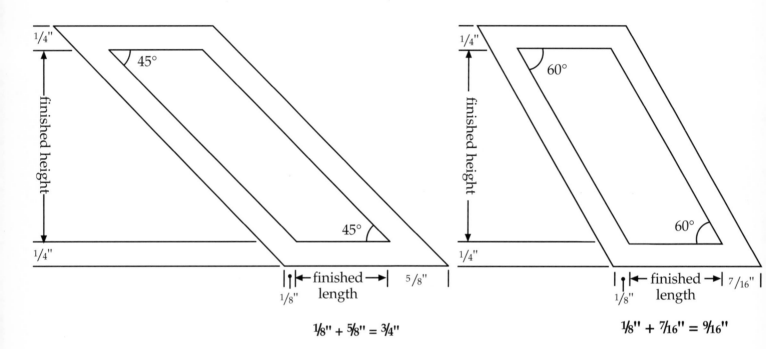

$$\text{1/8" + 5/8"} = \text{3/4"}$$

$$\text{1/8" + 7/16"} = \text{9/16"}$$

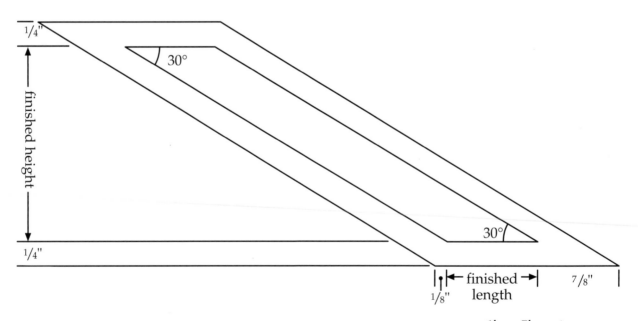

$$\text{1/8" + 7/8"} = \text{1"}$$

Try It Out: Cut a 60° parallelogram that has a finished height of 3¹/₄" and a finished length of 1".

1. Cut your fabric strip 3³/₄"w (*3¹/₄" finished height + ¹/₂"*).
2. Turn mat or strip so selvages are to your right.
3. Place ruler on strip with 60° line of ruler aligned with bottom edge of strip and make cut (**Fig. 25**). This will remove selvages and establish a 60° angle.

Fig. 25

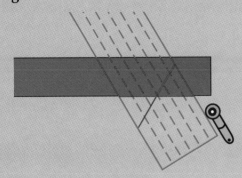

4. Turn strip or mat so that 60° edge is to your **left**. Measure 1⁹/₁₆" (*1" finished length + ⁹/₁₆"*) from top cut edge and mark (**Fig. 26**).

Fig. 26

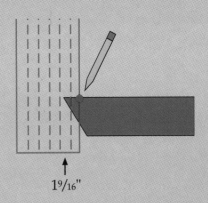

1⁹/₁₆"

5. Place ruler on strip with 60° line aligned with bottom edge of strip and right edge of ruler aligned with pencil mark; make cut (**Fig. 27**).

Fig. 27

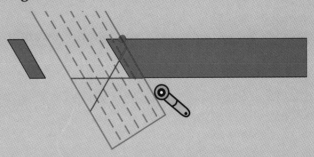

6. You now have a 60° parallelogram. When sewn into a block, this parallelogram will finish 3¹/₄"h and 1"l.

What They Are: Half rectangles are triangles made when a rectangle is cut in half diagonally.

Numbers You Need: To cut half rectangles, you must know the finished height and length of the triangle. As triangles vary in height and length, the amount to add allowing for seam allowances also varies. You must draft the finished triangle on graph paper and add $1/4$" seam allowances to know the size to cut your rectangle.

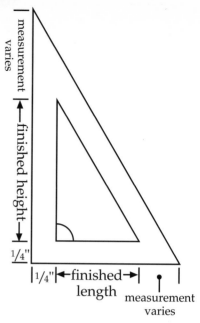

Try It Out: Cut a $1^1/2$" x $7/8$" finished half rectangle.

1. Draft the finished size half rectangle on graph paper. Add $1/4$" seam allowances and determine measurements (**Fig. 28**).

Fig. 28

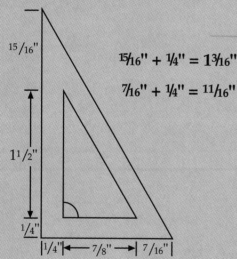

$$^{15}/_{16}" + ^1/_4" = 1^3/_{16}"$$

$$^7/_{16}" + ^1/_4" = 1^1/_{16}"$$

2. Cut your fabric strip $2^{11}/_{16}$" ($1^1/2$" *finished height* + $1^3/_{16}$").
3. Square up selvage end of strip and place squared-up end to your left.
4. Place ruler on strip with $1^9/_{16}$" measurement ($7/8$" *finished length* + $^{11}/_{16}$") aligned with left edge of strip and make cut (**Fig. 29**). You will have a rectangle that measures $2^{11}/_{16}$" x $1^9/_{16}$".

Fig. 29

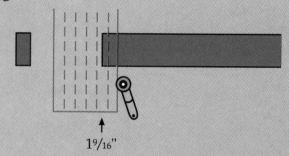

$1^9/_{16}$"

5. Place ruler diagonally on rectangle with edge of ruler aligned with opposite corners and make cut (**Fig. 30**).

Fig. 30

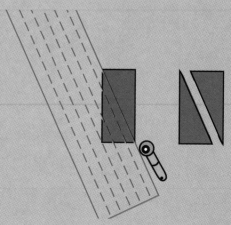

6. You now have 2 half rectangles measuring $2^{11}/_{16}$"h and $1^9/_{16}$"l. When sewn into a block, each half rectangle will finish $1^1/2$"h and $7/8$"l.

When piecing shapes such as equilateral triangles, parallelograms, or half rectangles, using a template to trim off points makes matching pieces easy.

Making a Template from a Pattern

Our full-sized template patterns have 2 lines: a solid cutting line that includes the 1/4" seam allowance and a dashed line showing the finished size of the piece.

1. Place a piece of tracing paper or template plastic over pattern and trace solid line. Make sure you transfer all alignment markings (dots) and grain line arrows and label templates.
2. Cut out template along drawn line. Check template against original pattern for accuracy.

Making Your Own Trimming Templates

You can make your own trimming templates from a quilt design you have drafted by using these general steps:

1. Draft full-size templates for each piece of a block onto graph paper and add the 1/4" seam allowance.
2. Cut out the templates.
3. Select templates for 2 pieces that will be sewn together; place templates with right sides together to determine what portion of a template to trim off to make piecing easier. Trim off excess portion of template (**Fig. 31**).

Fig. 31

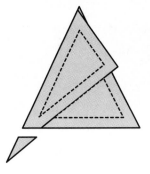

Using a Trimming Template

1. Cut out fabric piece(s) using your rotary cutter and ruler.
2. Place template right side down on wrong side of cutting ruler with trimmed corner even with the edge of the ruler. Tape the template to the ruler (**Fig. 32**).

Fig. 32

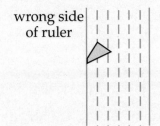

wrong side of ruler

3. Turn the ruler over and place ruler on right side of fabric piece, aligning template with fabric piece.
4. Place cutter against the right edge of the ruler and trim off fabric point (**Fig. 33**). If you have a large number of pieces to trim, you may stack several pieces and trim at the same time. Before cutting, make sure that all stacked pieces are right side up and all edges are aligned with the template.

Fig. 33

PIECING

Precise cutting followed by accurate piecing and careful pressing will ensure that all pieces of the quilt will fit together well. This section shares the basic sewing and pressing information you will need when piecing a quilt project.

GETTING STARTED

Set sewing machine stitch length for approximately 11 stitches per inch. Use a new needle suited for medium-weight woven fabric. Use a neutral-colored, general-purpose sewing thread (not quilting thread) in the needle and the bobbin. It is a good idea to fill several bobbins to have on hand while piecing. Check your bobbin periodically to keep from running out in the middle of a seam. Stitch first on scraps of fabric to check upper and bobbin thread tension; make any necessary adjustments.

When piecing, always place pieces right sides together and match raw edges. You will always use a 1/4" seam allowance (see **Performing a Sewing Test**, below). If using pins, remove the pins just before they reach the sewing machine needle. Do not sew over the pins; they may break or bend your needle, damage your machine, or cause fabric pieces to shift.

When machine sewing most pieces together, you do not have to backstitch — you sew from one end of the piece to the other end (see **Fig. 36**, pg. 23). When the next piece is added, the stitching lines will cross and the seam will be secured. The only time you will need to backstitch is when you are working with shapes such as diamonds and with set-in seams (see **Working with Diamonds and Set-in Seams**, pg. 23).

PERFORMING A SEWING TEST

Sewing accurately is as important as cutting accurately. After you have set the stitch length and tension on your machine, you should perform a sewing test to help you determine the correct size seam allowance to use when piecing. You will be using a 1/4" seam allowance to sew fabric pieces together, but when the seam allowance is pressed to 1 side you lose a slight amount of fabric. When more and more pieces are sewn together, this can make a big difference in the measurement of a block. To make up for the turned seam, **you actually sew a scant 1/4" seam allowance** (a seam that is slightly less than 1/4").

To perform a sewing test, follow these steps:

1. Refer to **Rotary Cutting**, pg. 8, to cut 3 strips of fabric that are exactly 1 1/2"w and about 6" to 8"l.
2. Using what you believe to be an accurate 1/4" seam allowance, sew the strips together along the long edges to form a strip set.
3. Press the seam allowances to 1 side.
4. Measure the width of the strip set. It should measure 3 1/2"w. Adjust your seam allowance until the strip set measures 3 1/2"w.

There are several ways to establish a sewing guide. You may use your presser foot as a guide if it will sew an accurate 1/4" seam allowance. If your presser foot cannot be used, you can make a guide for your machine by stacking several pieces of masking tape together on the throat plate of your machine (**Fig. 34**). There are also some companies that sell special 1/4" feet for sewing machines. It does not matter which method you use, as long as it allows you to sew accurately.

Fig. 34

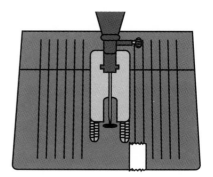

PRESSING

Pressing is an integral part of machine piecing — you press immediately after almost every seam you sew. You may find it helpful to move your ironing board close to your sewing chair and lower it to a height about even with your sewing machine table. This way you can turn and press seams without getting up and down.

Use an iron set on "cotton" for all pressing. You may find it helpful to use steam when pressing, but be careful not to get the fabric too wet, as it may stretch. Do not slide the iron on the fabric, since this may also stretch or distort pieces. Instead, pick up the iron and move it from one area of the fabric to another.

Seam allowances are almost always pressed to 1 side toward the darker fabric. This adds strength to the seam and helps to hide the seam allowance. However, to reduce bulk, it may be necessary to press seam allowances toward the lighter side, or on the rare occasion, to press them open. In order to prevent a dark seam allowance from showing through a light fabric, trim the darker seam allowance slightly narrower than the lighter seam allowance.

Press as you sew. When 2 pieces are sewn together, the seam allowance is almost always pressed before other pieces are added.

SEWING ACROSS SEAM INTERSECTIONS

When sewing across the intersection of 2 seams, place pieces right sides together and match seams exactly, making sure seam allowances are pressed in opposite directions (**Fig. 35**). To prevent fabric from shifting, you may wish to pin in place.

Fig. 35

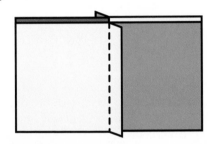

SEWING SHARP POINTS

To ensure sharp points when joining triangular or diagonal pieces, stitch across the center of the "X" (shown in pink) formed on the wrong side by previous seams (**Fig. 36**).

Fig. 36

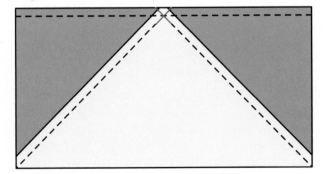

SEWING BIAS SEAMS

Care should be used when handling and stitching bias edges, since they stretch easily. After sewing the seam, carefully press seam allowance to 1 side, making sure not to stretch the fabric.

WORKING WITH DIAMONDS AND SET-IN SEAMS

Piecing diamonds and sewing set-in seams require special handling. You must use an accurate seam allowance, but you must also know where to start and stop each seam so that pieces can be set in as smoothly as possible. Using marking templates is an accurate way to mark these starting and stopping places. Follow the steps below to mark, then sew diamonds and set-in seams.

Using Marking Templates

Our full-sized marking template patterns have 2 lines: a solid cutting line, which includes the 1/4" seam allowance, and a dashed line showing the finished size of the piece. There are also dots on the template patterns to mark the beginning and end of stitching lines. (You can make your own templates by drafting the pattern pieces onto paper and marking the seam allowances. Add dots to the templates where seams will meet.)

1. To make a template from a pattern, trace pattern onto a piece of tracing paper or template plastic. Cut out template. Check template against original pattern for accuracy.
2. Use a pencil (or a sharp instrument for a plastic template) to carefully make a hole through each dot on the template. The hole need only be big enough for the point of the marking tool to fit through.
3. Place the template right side down on the wrong side of the fabric piece. Use a marking tool to mark dots on the fabric piece.

Sewing Set-in Seams

1. Place 2 diamond pieces right sides together, carefully matching edges; pin. Stitch pieces together between dots, backstitching at beginning and end of seam (**Fig. 37**). This will allow you to pivot the piece and set in the next piece precisely.

Fig. 37

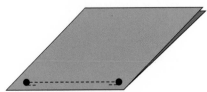

2. To sew first seam of the set-in piece, match right sides and pin the piece to the diamond on the left. Stitch seam from the outer edge to the dot, backstitching at the dot; clip threads (**Fig. 38**).

Fig. 38

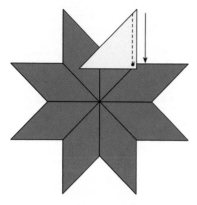

3. To sew the second seam, pivot the added piece to match raw edge of next diamond. Beginning with needle in the hole of the last stitch taken (at the dot), take 2 or 3 stitches, then backstitch, making sure not to backstitch into the previous seam allowance. Continue stitching to outer edge (**Fig. 39**).

Fig. 39

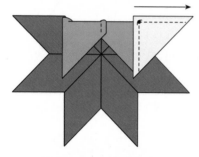

TRIMMING SEAM ALLOWANCES

When sewing shapes such as triangles or diamonds, some seam allowances may extend beyond the edges of the sewn pieces. Trim away "dog ears" that extend beyond the edges of the sewn pieces before adding additional pieces (**Fig. 40**).

Fig. 40

ADDING BORDERS

Borders cut along the lengthwise grain will lie flatter than borders cut along the crosswise grain. In most cases, our instructions for cutting borders for bed-size quilts include an extra 2" of length at each end for "insurance"; borders will be trimmed after measuring completed center section of quilt top.

Adding Squared Borders

1. Mark the center of each edge of quilt top.
2. Squared borders are usually added to top and bottom, then sides of the center section of a quilt top. To add top and bottom borders, measure across center of quilt top to determine length of borders (**Fig. 41**). Trim top and bottom borders to the determined length.

Fig. 41

3. Mark center of 1 long edge of top border. Matching center marks and raw edges, pin border to quilt top, easing in any fullness; stitch. Press seam allowance toward border strip. Repeat for bottom border. Do not stretch or force borders to fit.
4. Measure center of quilt top, including attached borders (**Fig. 42**). Trim side borders to the determined length.

Fig. 42

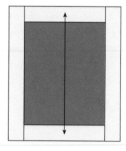

5. Mark center of 1 long edge of 1 side border. Matching center marks and raw edges, pin border to quilt top, easing in any fullness; stitch. Press seam allowance toward border strip. Repeat for remaining side border.

Adding Mitered Borders

1. Mark the center of each edge of quilt top.
2. Mark center of 1 long edge of top border. Measure across center of quilt top (see **Fig. 41**, pg. 24). Matching center marks and raw edges, pin border to center of quilt top edge. From center of border, measure out 1/2 the width of the quilt top in both directions and mark. Match marks on border with corners of quilt top and pin. Easing in any fullness, pin border to quilt top between center and corners. Sew border to quilt top, beginning and ending seams **exactly** 1/4" from each corner of quilt top and backstitching at beginning and end of stitching (**Fig. 43**).

Fig. 43

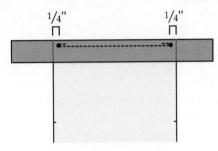

3. Repeat Step 2 to sew bottom, then side borders to center section of quilt top. To temporarily move first 2 borders out of the way, fold and pin ends as shown in **Fig. 44**. Press seam allowances toward border strips.

Fig. 44

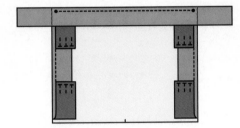

4. Lay quilt top right side down on a flat surface. Overlap top and bottom border strips over side border strips.
5. Mark bottom border strip on outer edge at the point where strips overlap (**Fig. 45**).

Fig. 45

6. Matching right sides and raw edges, bring border strips together with marked border strip on top. Use ruler to draw a line from the mark on the outer edge of border strip to the end of the stitching line (**Fig. 46**).

Fig. 46

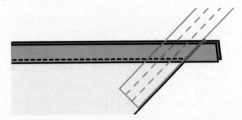

7. Pin border strips together along drawn line. (If you are working with a border that is a strip set, make sure seams of strips match. Place a pin through drawn line at each seam and make sure the pin goes through each seam on the bottom strip; pin strips together.) Sew directly on drawn line, backstitching at beginning and end of seam (**Fig. 47**).

Fig. 47

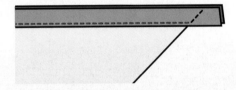

8. Turn mitered corner right side up. Check to make sure corner will lie flat with no gaps or puckers. If working with a border that is a strip set, make sure seams match. If necessary, use seam ripper to remove seam; carefully pin and sew seam again.
9. Trim seam allowances to 1/4"; press to 1 side.
10. Repeat Steps 4 - 9 to miter each remaining corner.

TECHNIQUES

Many of these time-saving techniques seem to work as if by magic! Combining simple sewing steps with rotary cutting techniques allows you to speedily piece some of the basic blocks and units found in many quilts.

CHAIN PIECING

Chain piecing whenever possible will make your work go faster, save thread, and will usually result in more accurate piecing.

1. Stack the pieces you will be sewing together beside your machine in the order you will need them and in a position that will allow you to pick them up easily.
2. Pick up each pair of pieces, carefully place them together as they will be sewn, and feed them into the machine one after the other. Stop between each pair only long enough to pick up the next and do not cut thread between pairs (**Fig. 48**).

Fig. 48

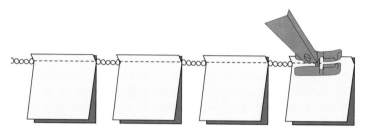

3. After all pieces are sewn, cut threads, press, and go on to the next step.

SEWING STRIP SETS

To help avoid distortion when sewing more than 2 strips together into a strip set, sew the first seam in one direction, then sew the next seam in the opposite direction (**Fig. 49**).

Fig. 49

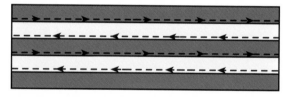

MAKING HALF-SQUARE TRIANGLE UNITS

What They Are: Square units made up of 2 half-square triangles are called half-square triangle units. When you are making more than a few units, using the grid method is quicker and as accurate as sewing individual triangles together. To use the grid method, you will draw a grid of squares on the lighter of 2 pieces of fabric, stitch the pieces together, then cut them apart to produce the units.

Numbers You Need: There are several numbers you need to know in order to use the grid method:

Size of the squares in the grid: Add ⁷/₈" to the finished height of the unit and ⁷/₈" to the finished length of the unit.

Number of squares needed in the grid: Since each square in the grid will make 2 units, divide the total number of units needed by 2. Round up the number to the next whole number if necessary.

Size of fabric pieces needed: First, determine the number of rows of squares you need. If you need 12 squares in a grid, 3 rows of 4 squares would be easy to work with. If the number of squares needed doesn't make a very good grid, simply add a few squares. For example, if you need 22 squares, make a grid of 24 squares with 4 rows of 6 squares. There is no specific rule to determine how you lay out the grid.

Second, multiply the number of rows in the grid by the size of the squares; add at least 1¹/₂". Repeat for the number of columns in the grid. Keep in mind that it is easier to work with fabric pieces that are about 18" x 21" or smaller.

Try It Out: Make twelve 2" x 2" finished half-square triangle units.

1. To make 12 units, you need a grid of 6 squares. Arrange the squares in 2 rows of 3 squares. Each square will measure 2⅞" *(2" finished height + ⅞")*. Cut 2 pieces of fabric 7¼" x 10¼" *(2 squares x 2⅞" + at least 1½" and 3 squares x 2⅞" + at least 1½")*.

2. Draw the grid of squares on the wrong side of the lighter fabric (**Fig. 50**).

Fig. 50

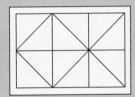

2⅞"

2⅞"

3. Draw a diagonal line through each square using one of the following methods.

Method 1: Drawing the diagonal lines as shown in **Fig. 51** will allow you to sew continuously around the grid, pivoting at the corners. Depending on the size of the grid, you may not always be able to stitch in a single line.

Fig. 51

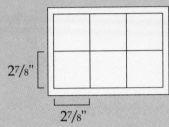

Method 2: Drawing the diagonal lines as shown in **Fig. 52** will allow you to sew straight across the grid, beginning and ending stitching on each row.

Fig. 52

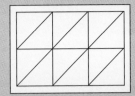

4. Place dark and light fabric pieces right sides together. Sew ¼" on each side of diagonal lines. For accuracy, it may be helpful to first draw your stitching lines onto the fabric, especially if your presser foot is not your ¼" guide. Project instructions include a diagram similar to **Fig. 53**, which shows stitching lines and the direction of the stitching.

Fig. 53

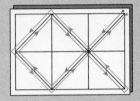

5. Use your rotary cutter and ruler to cut along all drawn lines of the grid. Each square will produce 2 half-square triangle units.

Fig. 54

6. Carefully press triangle units open, pressing seam allowance toward darker fabric. You now have twelve 2½" x 2½" half-square triangle units. When sewn into a block, each unit will finish 2" x 2".

MAKING QUARTER-SQUARE TRIANGLE UNITS

What They Are: These square units are made up of 4 quarter-square triangles. Quarter-square triangle units may be quickly made by sewing 2 half-square triangle units together that were made using the grid method.

Numbers You Need: There are 2 numbers you need in order to make the units.

Size of the squares in the grid: Add 1¼" to the finished height of the unit and 1¼" to the finished length of the unit.

Number of squares needed in the grid: You need the same number of squares in the grid as you need finished quarter-square triangle units.

Try It Out: Make six 2" x 2" finished quarter-square triangle units.

1. Drawing a grid of six 3¼" squares (*2" finished size + 1¼"*), follow Steps 1 - 6 of **Making Half-Square Triangle Units**, pg. 27, to make 12 half-square triangle units.

2. Place 2 half-square triangle units right sides and opposite colors together, matching seams (**Fig. 55**). Draw a diagonal line from corner to corner, then sew ¼" on each side of drawn line (**Fig. 56**). Cut on drawn line to make 2 quarter-square triangle units (**Fig. 57**). Repeat with remaining half-square triangle units.

Fig. 55   **Fig. 56**   **Fig. 57**

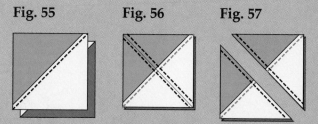

3. Carefully press each triangle unit open, pressing seam allowance to 1 side. You will have six 2½" x 2½" quarter-square triangle units. When sewn into a block, each unit will finish 2" x 2".

----------------------- **MAKING SNOWBALL BLOCKS** -----------------------

What They Are: Snowball blocks are square blocks with triangles at each corner. They are often used alternately with other blocks to create a beautiful design in a quilt. The corner triangles may be small or large depending on the block you wish to create. Traditionally, the blocks are pieced with an octagon shape and 4 triangles. The following speed-piecing method allows you to sew the blocks quickly and accurately using a large square and 4 small squares.

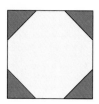

Numbers You Need: To cut your large square, add ½" to the finished height and ½" to the finished length of the block. To cut your 4 small squares, add ½" to the finished height and ½" to the finished length of the triangles.

Try It Out: Make a finished 9" Snowball block with 3" triangles at the corners.

1. Cut a large square 9½" x 9½" from 1 fabric (*9" finished size of the block + ½"*).
2. Cut 4 squares 3½" x 3½" from another fabric (*3" finished size of the triangle + ½"*).
3. Place 1 small square on each corner of large square with right sides together (**Fig. 58**). Stitch diagonally across small squares (**Fig. 59**). Trim ¼" from stitching lines (**Fig. 60**). Press open, pressing seam allowance toward darker fabric.

Fig. 58

Fig. 59

Fig. 60

4. You now have a 9½" x 9½" Snowball block. When sewn into a quilt, the block will finish 9" x 9".

What They Are: Geese units, representing geese in flight, are traditionally pieced using 2 small triangles and a large triangle. You can piece the units quickly and accurately using a rectangle and 2 squares.

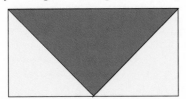

Numbers You Need: To use this method, the finished length of the unit **must** be 2 times the finished height of the unit (1" x 2", 3" x 6", etc.). To cut your rectangle, add 1/2" to the finished height of the unit and 1/2" to the finished length of the unit. To cut your 2 squares, add 1/2" to the finished height of the unit.

Try It Out: Make a finished 1" x 2" geese unit.

1. Cut a rectangle 1½" x 2½" from 1 fabric (*1" finished height + ½" and 2" finished length + ½"*).
2. Cut 2 squares 1½" x 1½" from another fabric (*1" finished height + ½"*).
3. Place 1 square on the rectangle and stitch diagonally as shown in **Fig. 61**. You may wish to draw a line across the square to use as a sewing guide. Trim ¼" from stitching line as shown in **Fig. 62**. Press open, pressing seam allowance toward darker fabric (**Fig. 63**).

Fig. 61

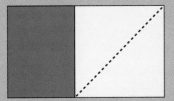

Fig. 62

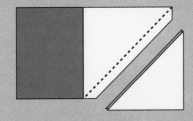

Fig. 63

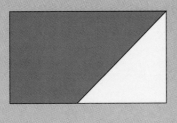

4. Place the second square on the opposite end of the rectangle. Stitch diagonally (**Fig. 64**). Trim ¼" from stitching line (**Fig. 65**). Press open, pressing seam allowance toward darker fabric (**Fig. 66**).

Fig. 64

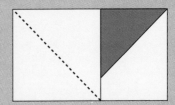

Fig. 65

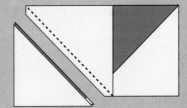

Fig. 66

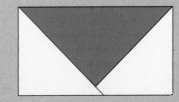

5. You now have a 1½" x 2½" geese unit. When sewn into a block, the unit will finish 1" x 2".

What They Are: These units look like squares set on point inside other squares. Like the geese unit, the square-in-a-square unit can be sewn using squares instead of triangles, thus avoiding sewing bias edges.

Numbers You Need: To cut your large center square, add ½" to the finished height of the unit and ½" to the finished length of the unit. To cut your small squares, divide the finished height of the unit by 2 and add ½"; divide the finished length of the unit by 2 and add ½".

Try It Out: Make a 2" x 2" finished square-in-a-square unit.

1. Cut 1 square 2½" x 2½" from 1 fabric (2" *finished height + ½" and 2" finished length + ½"*).

2. Cut 4 squares 1½" x 1½" from another fabric (2" *finished height divided by 2 + ½" and 2" finished length divided by 2 + ½"*).

3. Place 1 small square on 1 corner of large square with right sides together and stitch diagonally (**Fig. 67**). You may wish to draw a line diagonally across the square as a sewing guide. Trim ¼" from stitching line (**Fig. 68**). Press open, pressing seam allowance toward darker fabric (**Fig. 69**).

Fig. 67   **Fig. 68**

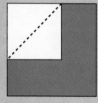   

Fig. 69

4. Place another small square on next corner of large square and stitch diagonally (**Fig. 70**). Trim ¼" from stitching line (**Fig. 71**). Press open, pressing seam allowance toward dark fabric. Repeat for remaining corners to complete square-in-a-square unit (**Fig. 72**).

Fig. 70   **Fig. 71**

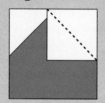   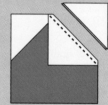

Fig. 72

5. You now have a 2½" x 2½" square-in-a-square unit. When sewn into a block, the unit will finish 2" x 2".

What They Are: Log Cabin blocks are made up of a center square (representing the chimney) and outer strips (representing the logs). Although Log Cabin blocks can be made in an assortment of sizes with almost any number of logs, most blocks can be quickly pieced using rotary-cut strips and assembly-line piecing.

Numbers You Need: For the center square (chimney), cut fabric strips the finished width + 1/2". A common finished center square size is twice the finished width of the logs. For logs, cut fabric strips the finished width + 1/2".

Try It Out: Make 3" Log Cabin blocks with 3/4" x 3/4" finished center squares and twelve 3/8"w finished logs.

1. Cut a strip of fabric 1¼"w *(3/4" finished width + 1/2")* for center squares.
2. Cut a 7/8"w strip *(3/8" finished width + 1/2")* from each of 6 light fabrics and 6 dark fabrics.
3. Sew 1¼"w strip and one 7/8"w light strip together into a strip set. Cut strip set at 1¼" intervals *(3/4" finished width of center square + 1/2")* to make desired number of units (**Fig. 73**). (You need 1 unit for each block.)

Fig. 73

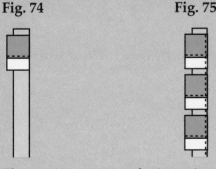

1¼"

4. Place 1 unit near 1 end of another light strip, matching right sides and raw edges (**Fig. 74**). Sew unit to strip but **do not** remove fabric from machine and **do not** cut strip. Place a second unit on strip close to first unit and continue sewing (**Fig. 75**). Repeat with remaining units.

Fig. 74   **Fig. 75**

5. Place strip on mat and trim strip even with edges of each unit (**Fig. 76**). Press seam allowances away from the center squares. (You will press all seam allowances away from the center.)

Fig. 76

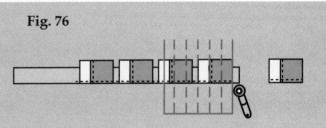

6. Referring to **Fig. 77**, rotate each unit and place it on a dark strip so that the last strip sewn is at the bottom. Repeat Steps 4 and 5 to add another log to units (**Fig. 78**).

Fig. 77   **Fig. 78**

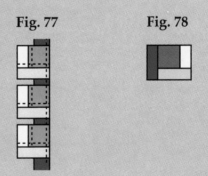

7. Rotate each unit and place it on another dark strip so that the last strip sewn is at the bottom. Repeat the same sewing, trimming, and pressing process (**Fig. 79**).

Fig. 79

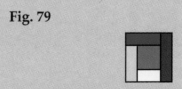

8. Continue to add logs to blocks, alternating 2 light, then 2 dark strips until all 12 strips have been used.
9. You will have 3½" Log Cabin blocks. When sewn into a quilt, each block will finish 3" x 3".

31

FINISHING

This section contains the information you need to complete your project. The basics of quilting, including marking the top, selecting and preparing the batting and backing, layering the quilt, and hand quilting are discussed. Once your project has been quilted, we show you how to make and attach bias or straight-grain binding with either mitered or overlapped corners. Instructions for adding a hanging sleeve are provided, as well as tips for labeling your project.

QUILTING

Quilting holds the layers (top, batting, and backing) of a quilt together and may be done by hand or machine. The project instructions show you quilting diagrams that can be used as suggestions for marking quilting designs. Because marking, layering, and quilting are interrelated, please read this entire section, pgs. 32 - 37, before beginning the quilting process on your project.

Several quilting types are shown in diagrams in the project instructions. Blue lines close to seamlines indicate "in the ditch" quilting. When quilting in the ditch, quilt on the side opposite the seam allowance. Blue lines a short distance from seamlines represent "outline" quilting. This is quilting approximately 1/4" from a seam. The blue decorative lines represent "ornamental" quilting.

Marking Quilting Lines
CHOOSING MARKING TOOLS
Fabric marking tools are often the subject of lively conversations. Quilters have strong opinions about the types of marking tools they use. It is impossible to recommend only one, since different marking tools work well for different applications.

Fabric marking pencils, various types of chalk markers, and soapstone markers are readily available to a quilter. A mechanical pencil works well on light-colored fabrics and is very helpful because the point is always sharp, allowing you to make a thin, clear line. There are mechanical pencils made especially for quilters with lead that is made to wash out of fabric. You may use regular pencil lead, but press down only as hard as necessary or the lines may be difficult to remove. Washable graphite pencils may be a good choice if you have trouble seeing the marks on light fabric. They make a larger, darker mark that will wash

away, but you must sharpen the pencil often. White pencils, soapstone markers, and some chalk markers work well on dark-colored fabrics. Silver and yellow pencils show up well on many colors. Since chalk rubs off easily, it is a good choice if you are marking as you quilt.

Test different marking tools on scraps of the fabric you will be quilting **before** you mark your quilt. If you cannot see the marks or if marks are not easily removed, use another marking tool.

USING QUILTING STENCILS
A wide variety of pre-cut quilting stencils, as well as entire books of quilting patterns, are available at your local quilt shop or fabric store. The patterns for some of the quilting designs used in this book are given on pgs. 90 - 94. Wherever you draw your quilting inspiration from, using a stencil makes it easy to mark intricate or repetitive designs on your quilt top. It is also helpful to have a stencil of a quilting design while you are quilting. If your marked lines fade or rub off, you may use your stencil to reapply the design to the quilt.

1. To make a stencil from a pattern, center template plastic over pattern and use a permanent marker to trace pattern onto plastic.
2. Use a craft knife to cut narrow slits along traced lines (**Fig. 80**).

Fig. 80

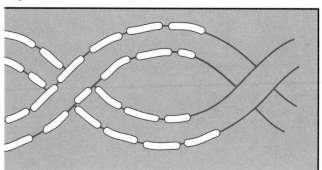

3. Use desired marking tool and stencil to mark quilting lines.

USING A LIGHT SOURCE
If you are marking on light-colored fabric, you may be able to trace your quilting design onto the fabric. Tape your quilting design to a sunny window or glass door. Place your fabric over the design and trace. Be sure the marking tool you use will last through the quilting process and not rub off.

Choosing and Preparing the Backing

To allow for slight shifting of the quilt top during quilting, the backing should be approximately 4" larger on all sides for a quilt or approximately 2" larger on all sides for a wall hanging. If you are making a bed-size quilt, using 90"w or 108"w fabric for the backing may eliminate piecing. Avoid using sheets for backing; the high thread count makes them hard to quilt. Your backing fabric should be equal in weight and quality to your quilt top. To piece a backing using 45"w fabric, use the following instructions.

1. Measure length and width of quilt top; add 8" (4" for a wall hanging) to each measurement.

2. If quilt top is 71"w or less, cut backing fabric into 2 lengths slightly longer than the determined **length** measurement (*length + 8" for a quilt or length + 4" for a wall hanging*). Trim selvages. Place lengths right sides together and sew long edges together, forming a tube (**Fig. 81**). Match seams and press along 1 fold (**Fig. 82**). Cut along pressed fold to form a single piece (**Fig. 83**).

Fig. 81

Fig. 82

Fig. 83

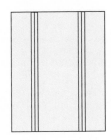

3. If quilt top is more than 71"w, cut backing fabric into 3 lengths slightly longer than the determined **width** measurement (*width + 8" for a quilt or width + 4" for a wall hanging*). Trim selvages. Sew long edges together to form a single piece (**Fig. 84**).

Fig. 84

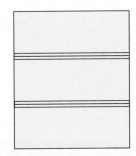

4. Trim backing to correct size, if necessary, and press seam allowances open.

Choosing and Preparing the Batting

Choosing the right batting will make your quilting job easier, but making the choice may seem overwhelming. Batting is available with many different fiber contents and in many different lofts or thicknesses. You will want to take into account the feel and look you desire and how much quilting you want to do.

A low-loft batting will give your quilt a flatter, thinner look. A high-loft batting gives your quilt a puffier look.

Bonded polyester batting is one of the most popular batting types. It is treated to stabilize the fibers and reduce "bearding," a process where batting fibers work their way out through the quilt fabric. Polyester batting does not have to be quilted closely, and many quilters find that it is easy to quilt, since the needle will work through the layers easily. Some quilters choose 100% cotton batting to give their quilts a wrinkled and antique look. Another favorite is cotton/polyester batting, which combines the best of both polyester and cotton battings. Batting is also available in wool and silk.

Whichever batting you choose, read the manufacturer's instructions closely for any special notes on care or preparation. Measure your quilt top before you go to buy your batting. You will need to purchase batting that is at least 8" wider and 8" longer than your quilt top. When you are ready to use your chosen batting in a project, cut the batting the same size as the prepared backing.

Layering the Quilt

1. Examine the wrong side of the quilt top closely; trim any seam allowances and clip any threads that may show through the front of the quilt. Press quilt top.
2. If quilt top is to be marked before layering, mark quilting lines (see **Marking Quilting Lines**, pg. 32).
3. Place backing **wrong** side up on a flat surface. Use masking tape to tape edges of backing to surface. Place batting on top of backing. Smooth batting gently, being careful not to stretch or tear. Center quilt top **right** side up on batting.
4. If hand quilting, pin layers together, placing pins approximately 4" apart and smoothing out fullness. Remove tape and turn the quilt over and check to make sure there are no puckers. Begin in the center and work toward the outer edges to hand baste all layers together. Use long stitches and place basting lines approximately 4" apart (**Fig. 85**). Make sure quilt is smooth and free from wrinkles. Baste 1/4" from outer edges of quilt. This will secure the edges of the quilt while the binding is being attached. A spoon is helpful for catching the tip of the needle on the quilt top when basting.

Fig. 85

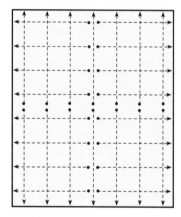

Hand Quilting

The quilting stitch is a basic running stitch that forms a broken line on the quilt top and backing. Stitches on the quilt top and backing should be straight and equal in length.

1. Secure center of quilt in a hoop or frame. Check quilt top and backing to make sure they are smooth. (It is very important to check the backing every time you move the hoop to assure that you will not quilt any wrinkles or puckers into the quilt.) To help prevent puckers, always begin quilting in the center of the quilt and work toward the outside edges.

2. Thread quilting needle with an 18" - 20" length of quilting thread; a longer length may tangle or fray. Do not double thread; make a small knot in one end. Using a thimble, insert needle into quilt top and batting approximately 1/2" from where you wish to begin quilting. Bring needle up at the point where you wish to begin (**Fig. 86**); when knot catches on quilt top, give the thread a quick, short pull to "pop" knot through fabric into batting (**Fig. 87**).

Fig. 86   **Fig. 87**

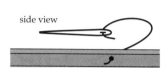

3. Holding the needle with your sewing hand and placing your other hand underneath the quilt, use thimble to push the tip of the needle down through all layers. As soon as needle touches your finger underneath, use that finger to push the tip only of the needle back up through the layers to the top of the quilt. (The amount of the needle showing above the fabric determines the length of the quilting stitch.) Referring to **Fig. 88**, rock the needle up and down, taking 3 - 6 stitches before bringing the needle and thread completely through the layers. Check the back of the quilt to make sure stitches are going through all layers. When quilting through a seam allowance or quilting a curve or corner, you may need to take 1 stitch at a time.

Fig. 88

4. When you reach the end of your thread, knot thread close to the fabric and "pop" knot into batting; carefully clip thread close to fabric.
5. Stop and move your hoop as often as necessary. You do not have to tie a knot every time you move your hoop; you may leave the thread dangling and pick it up again when you return to that part of the quilt.

BINDING

Binding encloses the raw edges of your quilt. It can be made by cutting strips of fabric on the straight grain or on the bias. Straight-grain binding may be used on projects that have straight sides and corners and will not be handled much. Bias binding wears better and lasts longer than binding cut on the straight grain. Bias binding can be eased around curves and corners; it also tends to lie flat. You should use bias binding if your project will be handled frequently or if you will be binding rounded corners.

Making Continuous Bias Strip Binding

When a long strip of binding is needed, the "continuous" method is quick and accurate.

1. Cut a square from binding fabric. (See **Determining Size of Square Needed for Bias Binding**, pg. 36, or project instructions.) Cut square in half diagonally to make 2 triangles.
2. With right sides together and using a 1/4" seam allowance, sew triangles together (**Fig. 89**); press seam allowances open.

Fig. 89

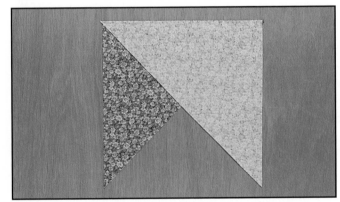

3. On wrong side of fabric, draw lines the width of the binding. Binding widths vary — 2 1/4" is a common size. Cut off any remaining fabric less than this width (**Fig. 90**).

Fig. 90

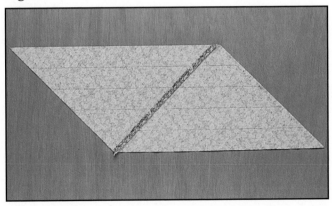

4. With right sides inside, bring short edges together to form a tube. Match raw edges so that first line of top section meets second drawn line of bottom section (**Fig. 91**). Carefully pin edges together by inserting pins through drawn lines at the point where the drawn lines intersect, making sure the pins go through intersections on both sides. For accuracy, you may find it helpful to draw a line 1/4" from raw edge. Using a 1/4" seam allowance, sew edges together. Press seam allowance open.

Fig. 91

5. To cut continuous strip, begin cutting along first drawn line (**Fig. 92**). Continue cutting along drawn line around tube.

Fig. 92

6. Trim ends of bias strip square.
7. Matching wrong sides and raw edges, press bias strip in half lengthwise to complete binding.

DETERMINING SIZE OF SQUARE NEEDED FOR BIAS BINDING

1. Measure the distance around the outside of the quilt; add 18" to determine the length of binding needed.
2. Multiply the length of binding needed by the binding width to determine the area of binding fabric needed.
3. Find the square root ($\sqrt{\ }$) of the area to determine the size of square to cut.

> **Formula**
> Length of binding x width of binding = area of binding
>
> $\sqrt{\text{area}}$ = size of square needed (round up to nearest whole number)

Making Straight-Grain Binding

1. To determine length of strip needed if attaching binding with mitered corners, measure edges of the quilt and add 18".
2. To determine lengths of strips needed if attaching binding with overlapped corners, measure each edge of quilt; add 3" to each measurement.
3. Cut lengthwise or crosswise strips of binding fabric the determined length and the desired width (2¼" is a common binding width). Strips may be pieced to achieve the necessary length.
4. Matching wrong sides and raw edges, press strip(s) in half lengthwise to complete binding.

Attaching Binding with Mitered Corners

1. Press 1 end of binding diagonally (**Fig. 93**).

Fig. 93

2. Lay binding around quilt to make sure that seams in binding will not end up at a corner. Adjust placement if necessary. Matching raw edges of binding to raw edge of quilt top and beginning with pressed end several inches from a corner, pin binding to right side of quilt along 1 edge. (The distance from the corner will vary depending on the size of your quilt. It may be only 4" or 5" on a small wall hanging and 20" to 24" on a larger quilt. You do not want the overlapped end to be at a corner or right in the middle of your quilt. Placing the overlap off center keeps it away from focal points.)

3. When you reach the first corner, mark ¼" from corner of quilt (**Fig. 94**).

Fig. 94

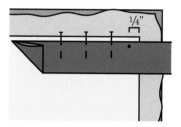

4. Using a ¼" seam allowance, sew binding to quilt, backstitching at beginning of stitching and when you reach the mark (**Fig. 95**). Lift needle out of fabric and clip threads.

Fig. 95

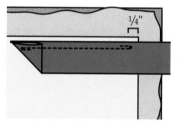

5. Fold binding as shown in **Figs. 96** and **97** and pin binding to adjacent side, matching raw edges. When you reach the next corner, mark ¼" from edge of quilt.

Fig. 96   **Fig. 97**

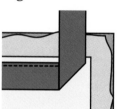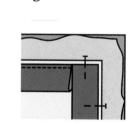

6. Backstitching at edge of quilt, sew pinned binding to quilt (**Fig. 98**); backstitch when you reach the next mark. Lift needle out of fabric and clip threads.

Fig. 98

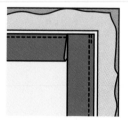

7. Repeat Steps 5 and 6 and continue sewing binding to quilt until binding overlaps beginning end by approximately 2". Trim excess binding.

8. Trim backing and batting even with edges of quilt top. (If you wish to add a hanging sleeve to your wall hanging or quilt, see **Making a Hanging Sleeve** before proceeding to Step 9.)

9. On 1 edge of quilt, fold binding over to quilt backing and pin pressed edge in place, covering stitching line (**Fig. 99**). On adjacent side, fold binding over, forming a mitered corner (**Fig. 100**). Repeat to pin remainder of binding in place.

Fig. 99   **Fig. 100**

10. Blindstitch binding to backing, taking care not to stitch through to front of the quilt.

Attaching Binding with Overlapped Corners

1. Trim backing and batting even with edges of quilt top.

2. Matching raw edges and using a ¼" seam allowance, sew a length of binding to top and bottom edges on right side of quilt.

3. Trim ends of binding even with edges of quilt top. Fold binding over to quilt backing and pin pressed edges in place, covering stitching line (**Fig. 101**); blindstitch binding to backing.

Fig. 101

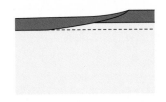

4. Leaving approximately 1½" of binding at each end, stitch a length of binding to each side edge of quilt.

5. Trim each end of binding ½" longer than bound edge. Fold each end of binding over to quilt backing (**Fig. 102**); pin in place. Fold binding over to quilt backing and blindstitch in place.

Fig. 102

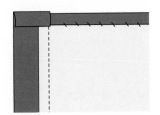

MAKING A HANGING SLEEVE

Attaching a hanging sleeve to the back of your wall hanging or quilt allows you to display your completed project on a wall or at a quilt show without damaging it. The hanging sleeve is attached before the binding is added.

1. Measure the width of the wall hanging or quilt top and subtract 1". Cut a piece of fabric 7"w by the determined measurement. For example, if your wall hanging measures 40"w, cut your fabric 7" x 39".

2. Press short edges of fabric piece ¼" to wrong side; press edges ¼" to wrong side again and machine stitch in place.

3. Matching wrong sides, fold piece in half lengthwise to form a tube.

4. Follow binding instructions to sew binding to quilt top and trim backing and batting. Before blindstitching binding to backing, match raw edges and stitch hanging sleeve to center top edge on back of wall hanging.

5. Finish binding wall hanging, treating the hanging sleeve as part of the backing.

6. Blindstitch bottom of hanging sleeve to backing, taking care not to stitch through to front of quilt.

7. Insert dowel or slat into hanging sleeve.

SIGNING AND DATING YOUR QUILT

Signing and dating your quilt is an important step in quiltmaking. Your completed quilt is a work of art and should be treated as such. And like any artist, you should sign and date your work. It will also let future generations know who made the quilt and when it was made.

There are many ways to do this — embroidering, cross stitching, making a muslin label and adding your information with a permanent marker, or using a purchased label. You should pick a method of signing and dating that reflects the style of the quilt, the occasion for which it was made, and your own particular talents.

PRACTICE MAKES PERFECT

Now that you know your quilting ABC's, come along and piece with ease! You can put your new abilities into practice with these charming projects that are based on old-fashioned favorites. The skills needed to complete each design are listed right at the beginning, so you'll know exactly which methods to review before taking the first step. Starting with the simplest techniques, the lessons progress to more challenging methods, making you a quilting graduate in no time!

PROJECT NO. 1
WINDY DAYS WALL HANGING

Easy methods make this Windy Days wall hanging a breeze to create! You'll use half-square triangles and strip sets to create the two block patterns — a traditional Pinwheel and a stylized Windmill. The blocks are offset with colorful Four-Patch and strip-set units.

Finished Wall Hanging Size: 32½" x 48½"
Finished Block Size: 8" x 8"

BEFORE YOU BEGIN

*We recommend that you read the entire **Quick Method ABC's** (pg. 4) before beginning this project to become familiar with rotary cutting and speed-piecing techniques. This project especially emphasizes the following skills:*

Cutting Squares (pg. 12)
Cutting Rectangles (pg. 13)
Cutting Half-Square Triangles (pg. 14)
Cutting Strip Sets (pg. 10)

YARDAGE

Yardage is based on 45"w fabric.

- ⅛ yd *each* of 4 blue prints
- ½ yd of cream print for block backgrounds
- ⅛ yd *each* of 4 red prints
- ⅛ yd *each* of 4 cream prints
- ⅜ yd of red solid
- ⅛ yd *each* of 4 tan prints
- ⅜ yd of blue solid
- 1¼ yds of tan print for borders
  1⅝ yds for backing
  ½ yd for hanging sleeve
  ¾ yd for binding
  36" x 52" batting

You will also need:
  assorted buttons

CUTTING

All cutting measurements include seam allowances.

1. **From *each* of 4 blue prints:**
   - Cut 1 strip 2⅞"w. From this strip, cut 4 squares 2⅞" x 2⅞". Cut squares once diagonally to make 8 **half-square triangles**.

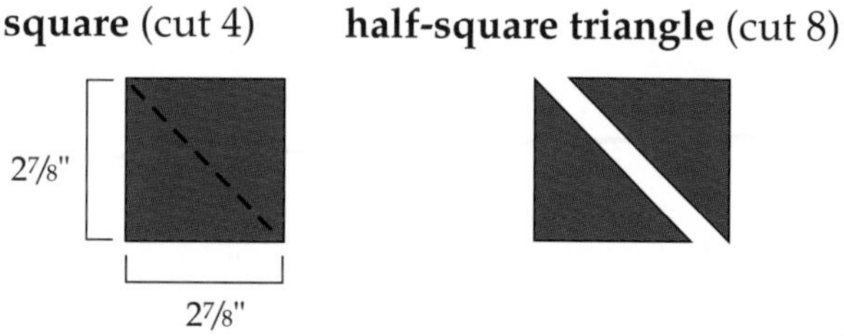

   2⅞" [diagram]
   2⅞"

   square (cut 4)   **half-square triangle** (cut 8)

   2⅞"
   2⅞"

2. **From cream print for block backgrounds:**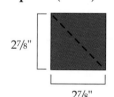
   - Cut 4 **strips** 1½"w.
   - Cut 2 strips 2⅞"w. From these strips, cut 16 squares 2⅞" x 2⅞". Cut squares once diagonally to make 32 **half-square triangles**.

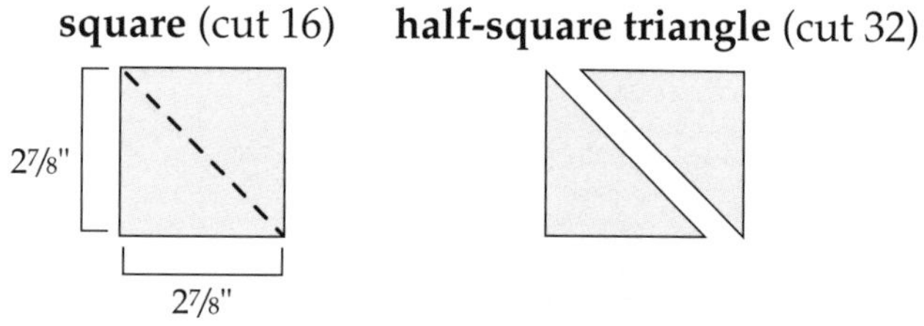

   square (cut 16)   **half-square triangle** (cut 32)

   2⅞"
   2⅞"

3. **From *each* of 4 red prints:**
   - Cut 1 **strip** 1½"w.

4. **From *each* of 4 cream prints:**
   - Cut 1 strip 2½"w. From this strip, cut 8 **rectangles** 2½" x 4½".

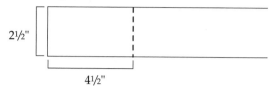

rectangle (cut 8)

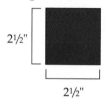

5. **From red solid:**
   - Cut 3 strips 2½"w. From these strips, cut 40 **squares** 2½" x 2½".

square (cut 40)

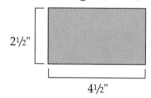

6. **From *each* of 4 tan prints:**
   - Cut 1 strip 2½"w. From this strip, cut 8 **rectangles** 2½" x 4½".

rectangle (cut 8)

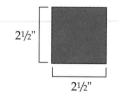

7. **From blue solid:**
   - Cut 3 strips 2½"w. From these strips, cut 36 **squares** 2½" x 2½".

square (cut 36)

8. **From tan print for borders:**
   - Cut 2 lengthwise strips 4½" x 40½" for **top/bottom borders**. Cut 2 lengthwise strips 4½" x 24½" for **side borders**.

PIECING

1. Place 1 blue print **half-square triangle** and 1 cream print **half-square triangle** right sides together. Sew triangles together along the long edge (**Fig. 1**). Press seam allowance toward the blue fabric to make **Unit 1**. Repeat with matching blue print **half-square triangles** to make a total of 8 **Unit 1's**.

Fig. 1   **Unit 1** (make 8)

2. Sew 2 **Unit 1's** together to make **Unit 2**. Make 4 **Unit 2's**.

Unit 2 (make 4)

3. Sew 2 **Unit 2's** together to make **Pinwheel Unit**. Make 2 **Pinwheel Units**.

Pinwheel Unit (make 2)

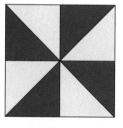

4. Repeat Steps 1 - 3 with each blue print to make a total of 8 **Pinwheel Units**.

5. Sew 1 red print **strip** and 1 cream print **strip** together to make 1 strip set. Cut strip set at 2½" intervals to make 8 **Unit 3's**.

Unit 3 (make 8)

6. Sew 2 **Unit 3's** together to make **Unit 4**. Make 4 **Unit 4's**.

Unit 4 (make 4)

7. Sew 2 **Unit 4's** together to make **Windmill Unit**. Make 2 **Windmill Units**.

Windmill Unit (make 2)

8. Repeat Steps 5 - 7 with each red print **strip** to make a total of 7 **Windmill Units**. (You will have some pieces left over.)
9. For Pinwheel Block, choose 4 matching cream print **rectangles**, 4 red solid **squares**, and 1 **Pinwheel Unit**.
10. Sew 2 **rectangles** and **Pinwheel Unit** together to make **Unit 5**.

Unit 5 (make 1)

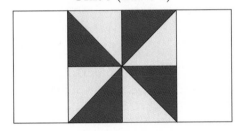

11. Sew 1 **rectangle** and 2 **squares** together to make **Unit 6**. Make 2 **Unit 6's**.

Unit 6 (make 2)

12. Sew **Unit 5** and **Unit 6's** together to complete **Pinwheel Block**.

Pinwheel Block

13. Repeat Steps 9 - 12 to make a total of 8 **Pinwheel Blocks**.
14. For Windmill Block, choose 4 matching tan print **rectangles**, 4 blue solid **squares**, and 1 **Windmill Unit**.
15. Sew 2 **rectangles** and **Windmill Unit** together to make **Unit 7**.

Unit 7 (make 1)

16. Sew 1 **rectangle** and 2 **squares** together to make **Unit 8**. Make 2 **Unit 8's**.

Unit 8 (make 2)

17. Sew **Unit 7** and **Unit 8's** together to complete **Windmill Block**.

Windmill Block

18. Repeat Steps 14 - 17 to make a total of 7 **Windmill Blocks**.

19. Sew 3 **Pinwheel Blocks** and 2 **Windmill Blocks** together to make **Row A**. Make 2 **Row A's**.

Row A (make 2)

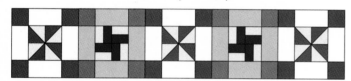

20. Sew 3 **Windmill Blocks** and 2 **Pinwheel Blocks** together to make **Row B**.

Row B (make 1)

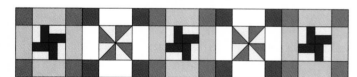

21. Referring to **Wall Hanging Top Diagram**, sew **Rows A** and **Row B** together to complete center design area of wall hanging.

22. Sew **top** and **bottom borders** to center design area.

23. Sew 2 red solid and 2 blue solid **squares** together to make **Unit 9**. Make 4 **Unit 9's**.

Unit 9 (make 4)

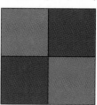

24. Sew 1 **Unit 9** to each end of each **side border**. Sew **side borders** to center design area to complete wall hanging top.

FINISHING

1. Follow **Quilting**, pg. 32, to mark, layer, and quilt using **Quilting Diagram** as a suggestion.

2. Referring to photo, sew buttons to wall hanging.

3. Piecing fabric as needed, follow **Making a Hanging Sleeve**, pg. 37, to make a hanging sleeve.

4. Cut a 22" square of binding fabric. Follow **Binding**, pg. 35, to bind wall hanging using 2¹/₄"w bias binding with mitered corners.

Quilting Diagram

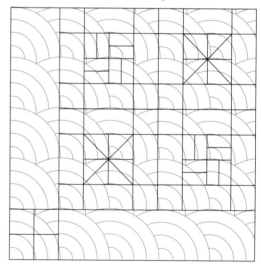

SHOOFLY LAP QUILT

Time will "shoo fly" when you're making this handsome lap quilt! The intriguing design is formed with simple Hourglass units and old-fashioned Shoofly blocks, all created using quarter-square triangles. Other pieced units are stitched with a quick grid technique. For a homey wall hanging, just add a hanging sleeve.

Finished Quilt Size: 59¹/₂" x 77¹/₂"
Finished Block Size: 9" x 9"

BEFORE YOU BEGIN

*We recommend that you read the entire **Quick-Method ABC's** (pg. 4) before beginning this project to become familiar with rotary cutting and speed-piecing techniques. This project especially emphasizes the following skills:*

Cutting Strip Sets (pg. 10)
Cutting Quarter-Square Triangles (pg. 15)
Making Half-Square Triangle Units (pg. 26)
Sewing Strip Sets (pg. 26)

YARDAGE

Yardage is based on 45"w fabric.

■ 3¹/₄ yds of brown plaid
■ 2 yds of tan print
■ 1¹/₄ yds of beige print
□ 1¹/₂ yds of light tan print
5 yds for backing
1 yd for binding
72" x 90" batting

CUTTING

All cutting measurements include seam allowances.

1. **From brown plaid:** ■
   - Cut 2 **strips** 3¹/₂"w.
   - Cut 2 strips 13"w. From these strips, cut 2 **rectangles** 13" x 25" for half-square triangle units.
   - Cut 2 lengthwise strips 7¹/₂" x 63¹/₂" for **top/bottom borders**.
   - Cut 2 lengthwise strips 7¹/₂" x 45¹/₂" for **side borders**.

2. **From tan print:**
   - Cut 4 strips 3¹/₂"w. From these strips, cut 36 **squares** 3¹/₂" x 3¹/₂".
   - Cut 2 strips 13"w. From these strips, cut 2 **rectangles** 13" x 25" for half-square triangle units.
   - Cut 4 **strips** 3¹/₂"w.

3. **From beige print:** ■
   - Cut 3 strips 10¹/₄"w. From these strips, cut 9 squares 10¹/₄" x 10¹/₄". Cut squares twice diagonally to make 36 **quarter-square triangles**. (You will need 34 and have 2 left over.)

square (cut 9)   **quarter-square triangle** (cut 36)

4. **From light tan print:** □
   - Cut 1 strip 7¹/₂"w. From this strip, cut 4 squares 7¹/₂" x 7¹/₂" for **border corner squares**.
   - Cut 3 strips 10¹/₄"w. From these strips, cut 9 squares 10¹/₄" x 10¹/₄". Cut squares twice diagonally to make 36 **quarter-square triangles**. (You will need 34 and have 2 left over.)

square (cut 9)   **quarter-square triangle** (cut 36)

PIECING

1. Place 1 brown plaid **rectangle** and 1 tan print **rectangle** right sides together. Referring to **Fig. 1**, follow **Making Half-Square Triangle Units**, pg. 26, to make 36 **half-square triangle units**. Repeat with remaining **rectangles** to make a total of 72 **half-square triangle units**.

Fig. 1

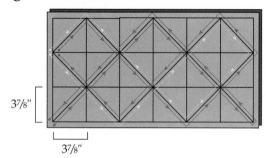

3⅞"

3⅞"

half-square triangle unit (make 72)

2. Sew 2 tan print **strips** and 1 brown plaid **strip** together to make **Strip Set**. Make 2 **Strip Sets**. Cut **Strip Sets** at 3½" intervals to make 18 **Unit 1's**.

Strip Set (make 2)

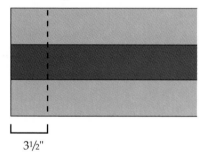

3½"

Unit 1 (make 18)

3. Sew 2 **half-square triangle units** and 1 tan print **square** together to make **Unit 3**. Make 36 **Unit 3's**.

Unit 3 (make 36)

4. Sew 2 **Unit 3's** and 1 **Unit 1** together to make **Shoofly Block**. Make 18 **Shoofly Blocks**.

Shoofly Block (make 18)

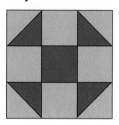

5. Sew 1 beige print **quarter-square triangle** and 1 light tan print **quarter-square triangle** together to make **Unit 2**. Make 34 **Unit 2's**.

Unit 2 (make 34)

6. Sew 2 **Unit 2's** together to make **Hourglass Block**. Make 17 **Hourglass Blocks**.

Hourglass Block (make 17)

7. Sew 3 **Shoofly Blocks** and 2 **Hourglass Blocks** together to make **Row A**. Make 4 **Row A's**.

Row A (make 4)

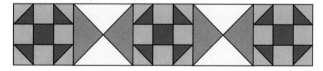

8. Sew 3 **Hourglass Blocks** and 2 **Shoofly Blocks** together to make **Row B**. Make 3 **Row B's**.

Row B (make 3)

46

9. Referring to **Quilt Top Diagram**, sew **Row A's** and **Row B's** together to complete center design area of quilt top.

10. Sew 1 **border corner square** to each end of **top/bottom borders**. Add **side**, then **top** and **bottom borders** to center design area to complete quilt top.

FINISHING

1. Follow **Quilting**, pg. 32, to mark, layer, and quilt using **Quilting Diagram** as a suggestion.
2. Cut a 28" square of binding fabric. Follow **Binding**, pg. 35, to bind quilt using 2¼"w bias binding with mitered corners.

Quilt Top Diagram

SNOWBALLS IN OHIO QUILT

To create traditional Ohio Stars, we used a grid method to make the quarter-square triangle units for the star points. The alternating Snowball blocks are super easy: simply sew small print squares to each corner of a large white square and trim along the seams.

Finished Quilt Size: 87¹/₂" x 105¹/₂"
Finished Block Size: 9" x 9"

BEFORE YOU BEGIN

*We recommend that you read the entire **Quick-Method ABC's** (pg. 4) before beginning this project to become familiar with rotary cutting and speed-piecing techniques. This project especially emphasizes the following skills:*

Cutting Lengthwise Strips (pg. 11)
Making Half-Square Triangle Units (pg. 26)
Making Quarter-Square Triangle Units (pg. 27)
Making Snowball Blocks (pg. 28)
Adding Mitered Borders (pg. 25)

YARDAGE

Yardage is based on 45"w fabric.

■ 6³/₈ yds of blue print

☐ 8¹/₈ yds of white print
8 yds for backing
1¹/₈ yds for binding
120" x 120" batting

CUTTING

All cutting measurements include seam allowances.

1. **From blue print:** ■
   - Cut 15 strips 3¹/₂"w. From these strips, cut 156 **squares** 3¹/₂" x 3¹/₂". (32 squares will be used for Ohio Star Blocks and 124 squares will be used for Snowball Blocks.)
   - Cut 2 strips 27"w. From these strips, cut 3 **rectangles** 19" x 27" for half-square triangle units.
   - Cut 4 lengthwise strips 2¹/₂" x 110" for **side inner** and **outer borders**.
   - Cut 4 lengthwise strips 2¹/₂" x 92" for **top/bottom inner** and **outer borders**.

2. **From white print:** ☐
   - Cut 8 strips 9¹/₂"w. From these strips, cut 31 **large squares** 9¹/₂" x 9¹/₂".
   - Cut 12 strips 3¹/₂"w. From these strips, cut 128 **small squares** 3¹/₂" x 3¹/₂".
   - Cut 2 strips 27"w. From these strips, cut 3 **rectangles** 19" x 27" for half-square triangle units.
   - Cut 2 lengthwise strips 8¹/₂" x 110" for **side middle borders**.
   - Cut 2 lengthwise strips 8¹/₂" x 92" for **top/bottom middle borders**.

PIECING

1. Place 1 white print **rectangle** and 1 blue print **rectangle** right sides together. Referring to **Fig. 1**, follow **Making Half-Square Triangle Units**, pg. 26, to make 144 **half-square triangle units**. (You will need 128 and have 16 left over.)

Fig. 1

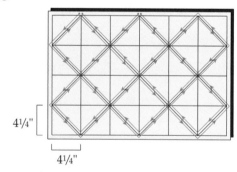

4¹/₄"

4¹/₄"

half-square triangle unit (make 144)

2. Follow Steps 2 and 3 of **Making Quarter-Square Triangle Units**, pg. 27, to make 128 **quarter-square triangle units**.

quarter-square triangle unit (make 128)

3. Sew 4 **quarter-square triangle units**, 4 white print **small squares**, and 1 blue print **square** together to make **Ohio Star Block**. Make 32 **Ohio Star Blocks**.

Ohio Star Block (make 32)

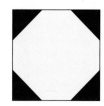

4. Using 4 blue print **squares** and 1 white print **large square**, follow Steps 1 - 4 of **Making Snowball Blocks**, pg. 28, to make **Snowball Block**. Make 31 **Snowball Blocks**.

Snowball Block (make 31)

5. Sew 4 **Ohio Star Blocks** and 3 **Snowball Blocks** together to make **Row A**. Make 5 **Row A's**.

Row A (make 5)

6. Sew 4 **Snowball Blocks** and 3 **Ohio Star Blocks** together to make **Row B**. Make 4 **Row B's**.

Row B (make 4)

7. Referring to **Quilt Top Diagram**, sew **Row A's** and **Row B's** together to make center design area of quilt top.
8. Sew 1 each of **side inner**, **middle**, and **outer border strips** together to make **Side Border Unit**. Make 2 **Side Border Units**. Repeat to make 2 **Top/Bottom Border Units**.

Border Unit

9. Follow **Adding Mitered Borders**, pg. 25, to sew **Border Units** to center design area to complete quilt top.

FINISHING
1. Follow **Quilting**, pg. 32, to mark, layer, and quilt using **Quilting Diagram** as a suggestion. **Heart Wreath** quilting pattern is on pg. 90.
2. Cut a 33" square of binding fabric. Follow **Binding**, pg. 35, to bind quilt using 2¹/₄"w bias binding with mitered corners.

Quilting Diagram

TIMBER RIDGE QUILT

Representing a tranquil knoll of evergreens, our classic Timber Ridge quilt will be a picturesque project for practicing your new skills. The tree "branches" are formed with rows of half-square triangle units that are pieced using a speedy grid method; other simple-to-piece units complete the blocks.

Finished Quilt Size: 84" x 104"
Finished Block Size: 12" x 12"

BEFORE YOU BEGIN

*We recommend that you read the entire **Quick-Method ABC's** (pg. 4) before beginning this project to become familiar with rotary cutting and speed-piecing techniques. This project especially emphasizes the following skills:*

Cutting Lengthwise Strips (pg. 11)
Making Half-Square Triangle Units (pg. 26)
Adding Squared Borders (pg. 24)

YARDAGE

Yardage is based on 45"w fabric.

▪ 6⅝ yds of green print
□ 7¾ yds of white print
■ ½ yd of brown print
7¾ yds for backing
1 yd for binding
120" x 120" batting

CUTTING

All cutting measurements include seam allowances.

1. **From green print:** ▪
    - Cut 9 strips 2½"w. From these strips, cut 24 **sashing A's** 2½" x 12½" and 2 **sashing B's** 2½" x 18".
    - Cut 3 strips 8⅞"w. From these strips, cut 9 squares 8⅞" x 8⅞". Cut squares once diagonally to make 18 half-square triangles for **large triangles**.
    - Cut 3 strips 22"w. From these strips, cut 5 **rectangles** 22" x 16" for half-square triangle units.
    - Cut 2 lengthwise strips 2½" x 108" for **side outer borders**.
    - Cut 2 lengthwise strips 2½" x 88" for **side inner borders**.
    - Cut 1 lengthwise strip 2½" x 88" for **sashing C**.
    - Cut 2 lengthwise strips 2½" x 84" for **top/bottom outer borders**.
    - Cut 2 lengthwise strips 2½" x 74" for **sashing D's**.
    - Cut 2 lengthwise strips 2½" x 64" for **top/bottom inner borders**.
    - Cut 2 lengthwise strips 2½" x 46" for **sashing E's**.

2. **From white print:** □
    - Cut 2 strips 18¼"w. From these strips, cut 3 squares 18¼" x 18¼". Cut squares twice diagonally to make 12 quarter-square triangles for **setting triangles**. (You will need 10 and have 2 left over.)
    - Cut 1 strip 9⅜"w. From this strip, cut 2 squares 9⅜" x 9⅜". Cut squares once diagonally to make 4 half-square triangles for **corner setting triangles**.
    - Cut 3 strips 22"w. From these strips, cut 5 **rectangles** 22" x 16" for half-square triangle units.
    - Cut 3 strips 2½"w. From these strips, cut 36 **squares** 2½" x 2½".
    - Cut 2 strips 7½"w. From these strips, cut 9 squares 7½" x 7½". Cut squares twice diagonally to make 36 **quarter-square triangles**.
    - Cut 2 lengthwise strips 8½" x 104" for **side middle borders**.
    - Cut 2 lengthwise strips 8½" x 68" for **top/bottom middle borders**.

3. **From brown print:** ■
    - Cut 2 strips 6½"w. From these strips, cut 18 **rectangles** 3" x 6½".

PIECING

1. To make half-square triangle units, place 1 white print **rectangle** and 1 green print **rectangle** right sides together. Referring to **Fig. 1**, follow **Making Half-Square Triangle Units**, pg. 26, to make 70 **half-square triangle units**. Repeat with remaining **rectangles** to make a total of 350 **half-square triangle units**. (You will need 324 and have 26 left over.)

Fig. 1

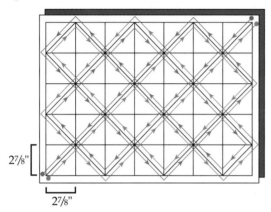

2⅞"
2⅞"

half-square triangle unit (make 350)

2. Sew 5 **half-square triangle units** and 1 **square** together to make **Unit 1**. Make 18 **Unit 1's**.

Unit 1 (make 18)

3. Sew 5 **half-square triangle units** and 1 **square** together to make **Unit 2**. Make 18 **Unit 2's**.

Unit 2 (make 18)

4. Sew 1 **Unit 1** and 1 **Unit 2** together to make **Unit 3**. Make 18 **Unit 3's**.

Unit 3 (make 18)

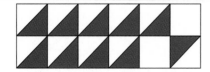

5. Sew 4 **half-square triangle units** together to make **Unit 4**. Make 36 **Unit 4's**.

Unit 4 (make 36)

6. Sew 2 **Unit 4's** together to make **Unit 5**. Make 18 **Unit 5's**.

Unit 5 (make 18)

7. Sew 2 **quarter-square triangles** and 1 **rectangle** together to make **Unit 6**. Make 18 **Unit 6's**.

Unit 6 (make 18)

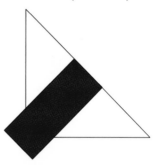

8. Sew 1 **large triangle** and 1 **Unit 6** together to make **Unit 7**. Make 18 **Unit 7's**.

Unit 7 (make 18)

9. Sew 1 each of **Unit 3**, **Unit 5**, and **Unit 7** together to make **Unit 8**. Make 18 **Unit 8's**.

Unit 8 (make 18)

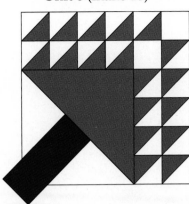

10. Referring to **Fig. 2**, trim **rectangle** even with 1 edge of **Unit 8**.

Fig. 2

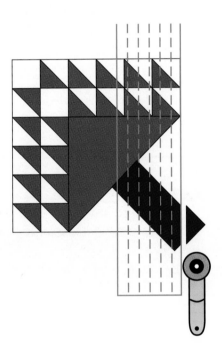

11. Referring to **Fig. 3**, trim **rectangle** even with adjacent edge of **Unit 8** to complete **Tree Block**.

Fig. 3

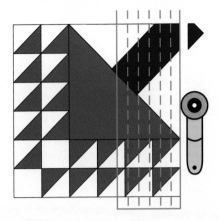

12. Repeat Steps 10 and 11 to complete a total of 18 **Tree Blocks**.

Tree Block (make 18)

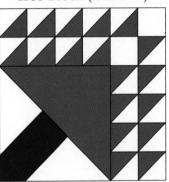

13. Referring to **Assembly Diagram**, pg. 57, sew **setting triangles**, **corner setting triangles**, **sashing A's - E's**, and **Tree Blocks** together into 6 diagonal **Rows**.

14. To make alignment marks on sashing, lay **Row 2** on a flat surface. Placing ruler along long edges of **sashing A's**, mark **sashing E** directly across from long edges (**Fig. 4**). Repeat to mark **sashing C, D,** and **E** on **Rows 3 - 6**.

Fig. 4

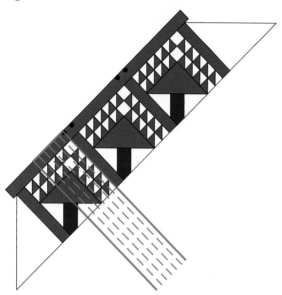

15. Match seamlines of **sashing A's** on **Row 1** with marks on **sashing E** of **Row 2**. Pin and sew **Rows 1** and **2** together. Repeat to attach remaining **Rows**.
16. Referring to **Fig. 5**, place ruler on quilt top with long edge of ruler aligned with raw edge of **setting triangle** and **corner setting triangle**. Use rotary cutter to trim edges of **sashings** even with edges of **setting triangles** and **corner setting triangles** to complete center design area of quilt top.

Fig. 5

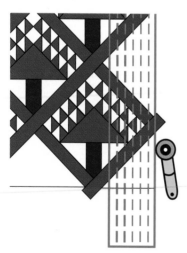

17. Follow **Adding Squared Borders**, pg. 24, to sew **top**, **bottom**, then **side inner borders** to center design area. Repeat to add **middle** and **outer borders** to complete quilt top.

FINISHING
1. Follow **Quilting**, pg. 32, to mark, layer, and quilt using **Quilting Diagram** as a suggestion. **Petal** quilting pattern is on pg. 91.
2. Cut a 33" square of binding fabric. Follow **Binding**, pg. 35, to bind quilt using $2^{1}/_{4}$"w bias binding with mitered corners.

Quilting Diagram

Quilt Top Diagram

56

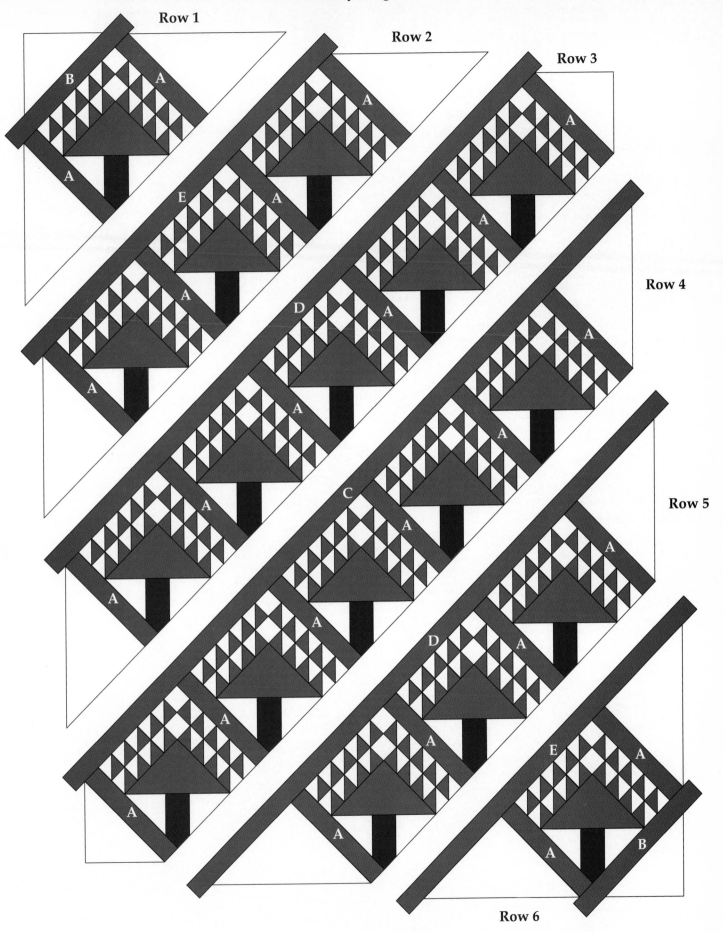

SCHOOLHOUSE WALL HANGING

With the quilting shortcuts you've learned, you'll actually have fun completing this homework assignment! Each piece of the Schoolhouse block is simple to rotary cut, and we provide handy trimming templates to make your piecing even easier. The center block is accented with a rustic border of easy Log Cabin units.

Finished Wall Hanging Size: 36" x 36"
Finished Block Size: 12" x 12"

BEFORE YOU BEGIN

*We recommend that you read the entire **Quick-Method ABC's** (pg. 4) before beginning this project to become familiar with rotary cutting and speed-piecing techniques. This project especially emphasizes the following skills:*

Cutting Parallelograms (pg.18)
Cutting Equilateral Triangles (pg. 16)
Cutting Half Rectangles (pg. 20)
Making Log Cabin Blocks (pg. 31)
Using Trimming Templates (pg. 21)

YARDAGE

Yardage is based on 45"w fabric.

- ☐ 1 yd of cream print
- ▨ ³/₄ yd of red print
- ■ ¹/₄ yd of navy solid
- ◪ ¹/₄ yd *each* of 6 blue prints and 6 tan prints
- ■ ⁵/₈ yd of red plaid
  1¹/₄ yds for backing
  ¹/₄ yd for hanging sleeve
  ³/₈ yd for binding
  40" x 40" batting

You will also need:
tracing paper or template plastic

CUTTING

All cutting measurements include seam allowances. Label pieces for easy identification.

1. **From cream print:** ☐
   - Cut 1 strip 1⁵/₈"w. From this strip, cut 1 square 1⁵/₈" x 1⁵/₈". Cut square once diagonally to make 2 half-square triangles for **B's**.
   - Cut 1 strip 2³/₄"w. From this strip, cut 1 rectangle 2³/₄" x 2³/₈" for **D** and 1 rectangle 2³/₄" x 9¹/₈" for **E**.

- Cut 1 strip 4⁷/₁₆"w. From this strip, cut 2 rectangles 4⁷/₁₆" x 2⁹/₁₆". Leaving rectangles stacked with wrong sides together, cut rectangles once diagonally to make 2 half rectangles for **F** and 2 reversed half rectangles for **Reverse F**. (You will need 1 of each and have 1 of each left over.)

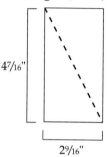

rectangle (cut 2)

4⁷/₁₆"

2⁹/₁₆"

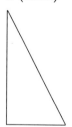

F (cut 2)

Reverse F (cut 2)

- Cut 1 strip 3³/₄"w. Referring to Steps 2 - 5 of **Cutting Parallelograms**, pg. 19, and **Fig. 1**, cut a 60° parallelogram 3³/₄" x 1⁹/₁₆" for **H**.

Fig. 1

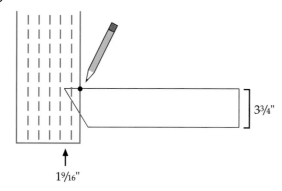

1⁹/₁₆"

- Cut 1 strip 1³/₄"w. From this strip, cut 1 rectangle 1³/₄" x 5¹/₂" for **K**.
- Cut 1 strip 1⁵/₈"w. From this strip, cut 2 rectangles 1⁵/₈" x 4" for **O's**.
- Cut 1 strip 1¹/₂"w. From this strip, cut 1 rectangle 1¹/₂" x 7³/₄" for **R** and 1 rectangle 1¹/₂" x 7" for **T**.
- Cut 1 strip 9³/₈"w. From this strip, cut 2 squares 9³/₈" x 9³/₈". Cut squares once diagonally to make 4 half-square triangles for **small corner triangles**.

2. **From red print:** ▪
   - Cut 1 strip 2³/₄"w. From this strip, cut 1 square 2³/₄" x 2³/₄". Cut square twice diagonally to make 4 quarter-square triangles. You will need 1 for **A** and have 3 left over.
   - Cut 1 strip 2"w. From this strip, cut 1 square 2" x 2" for **C**.
   - Cut 1 strip 4"w. Referring to Steps 2 - 4 of **Cutting Equilateral Triangles**, pg. 16, cut 1 equilateral triangle for **G**.

- Cut 1 strip 3³/₄"w. Referring to Steps 2 - 5 of **Cutting Parallelograms**, pg. 19, and **Fig. 2**, cut a 60° parallelogram 3³/₄" x 7¹³/₁₆" for **I**.

Fig. 2

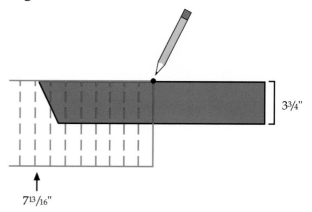

7¹³/₁₆"

- Cut 1 strip 1¹/₂"w. From this strip, cut 1 rectangle 1¹/₂" x 4¹/₄" for **J**.
- Cut 1 strip 1³/₄"w. From this strip, cut 2 rectangles 1³/₄" x 5¹/₂" for **L's**, 2 rectangles 1³/₄" x 4" for **P's**, and 1 rectangle 1³/₄" x 7³/₄" for **S**.
- Cut 1 strip 1"w. From this strip, cut 1 rectangle 1" x 4¹/₄" for **M**.
- Cut 1 strip 3"w. From this strip, cut 1 rectangle 3" x 4" for **N**.
- Cut 1 strip 1¹/₄"w. From this strip, cut 1 rectangle 1¹/₄" x 7³/₄" for **Q**.
- Cut 2 **strips** 1¹/₄"w.

3. **From navy solid:** ■
   - Cut 6 strips 1"w. From these strips, cut 2 **short inner borders** 1" x 17¹/₂", 2 **long inner borders** 1" x 18¹/₂", 2 **short outer borders** 1" x 24¹/₂", and 2 **long outer borders** 1" x 25¹/₂".

4. **From *each* blue print:** ▪
   - Cut 4 **strips** ⁷/₈"w.

5. **From *each* tan print:** ▪
   - Cut 4 **strips** ⁷/₈"w.

6. **From red plaid:** ■
   - Cut 1 strip 18⁵/₈"w. From this strip, cut 2 squares 18⁵/₈" x 18⁵/₈". Cut squares once diagonally to make 4 half-square triangles for **large corner triangles**.

PIECING

1. Sew 2 **B's**, **A**, and **C** together to make **Unit 1**.

Unit 1

2. Sew **D**, **E**, and **Unit 1** together to make **Row 1**.

Row 1

3. Use patterns, pgs. 66 and 67, and follow **Using Trimming Templates**, pg. 21, to make trimming templates for **F**, **Reverse F**, **G**, **H**, and **I**; use templates to trim pieces.

4. Sew **G**, **H**, and **I** together to make **Unit 2**.

Unit 2

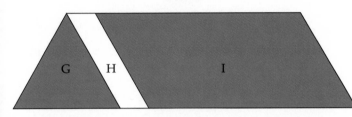

5. Sew **F**, **Reverse F**, and **Unit 2** together to make **Row 2**.

Row 2

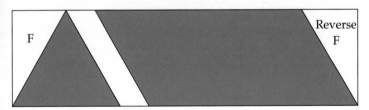

6. Sew 2 **L's** and **K** together to make **Unit 3**.

Unit 3

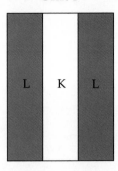

7. Sew **J**, **M**, and **Unit 3** together to make **Unit 4**.

Unit 4

8. Sew 2 **O's**, 2 **P's**, and **N** together to make **Unit 5**.

Unit 5

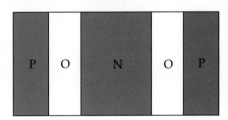

61

9. Sew **Q**, **R**, **S**, and **Unit 5** together to make **Unit 6**.

Unit 6

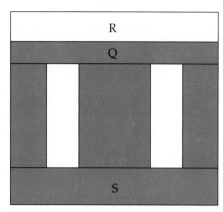

10. Sew **Unit 4**, **Unit 6**, and **T** together to make **Row 3**.

Row 3

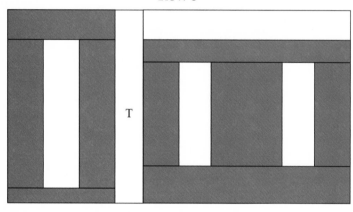

11. Sew **Rows 1**, **2**, and **3** together to make **Schoolhouse Block**.

Schoolhouse Block

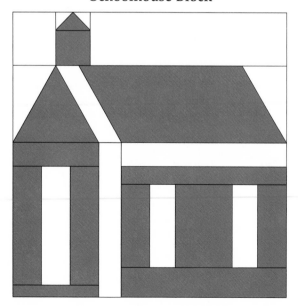

12. Referring to **Wall Hanging Top Diagram**, pg. 64, sew **small corner triangles** and **Schoolhouse Block** together.
13. Referring to **Wall Hanging Top Diagram**, sew navy **short inner borders** to opposite sides of wall hanging. Sew navy **long inner borders** to remaining sides.
14. To make Log Cabin Blocks, use red 1¼"w **strips** for center squares and tan and blue print ⅞"w **strips** for logs. Follow **Making Log Cabin Blocks**, pg. 31, to make 28 **Log Cabin Blocks**.

Log Cabin Block (make 28)

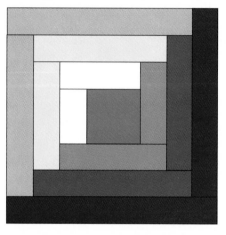

15. Sew 6 **Log Cabin Blocks** together to make **Top Left Border**. Sew 6 **Log Cabin Blocks** together to make **Bottom Right Border**.
16. Sew 8 **Log Cabin Blocks** together to make **Bottom Left Border**. Sew 8 **Log Cabin Blocks** together to make **Top Right Border**.

Top Left Border

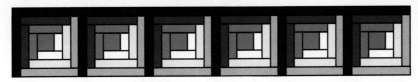

Bottom Right Border

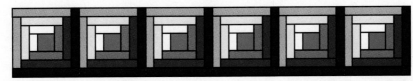

Bottom Left Border

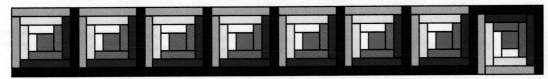

Top Right Border

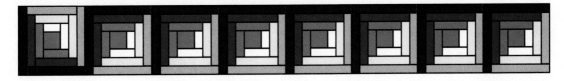

17. Referring to **Wall Hanging Top Diagram**, pg. 64, sew **Top Left** and **Bottom Right Borders** to wall hanging.
18. Sew **Bottom Left** and **Top Right Borders** to wall hanging.
19. Referring to **Wall Hanging Top Diagram**, sew navy **short outer borders** to opposite sides of wall hanging. Sew navy **long outer borders** to remaining sides of wall hanging.
20. Referring to **Wall Hanging Top Diagram**, add **large corner triangles** to complete wall hanging top.

FINISHING
1. Follow **Quilting**, pg. 32, to mark, layer, and quilt using **Quilting Diagram**, pg. 65, as a suggestion. **Clamshell** quilting pattern is on pg. 91.
2. Follow **Making a Hanging Sleeve**, pg. 37, to make a hanging sleeve.
3. Follow **Binding**, pg. 35, to bind wall hanging using 2¼"w straight-grain binding with overlapped corners.

63

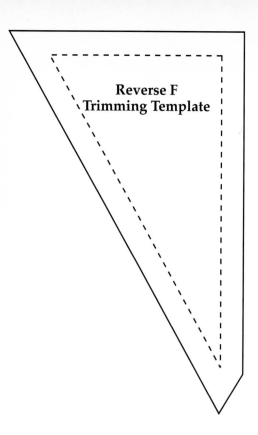

**Reverse F
Trimming Template**

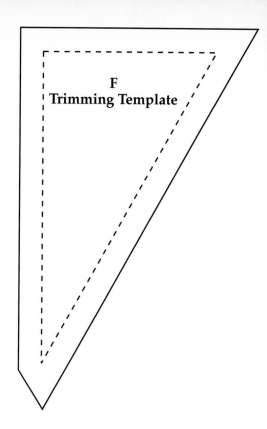

**F
Trimming Template**

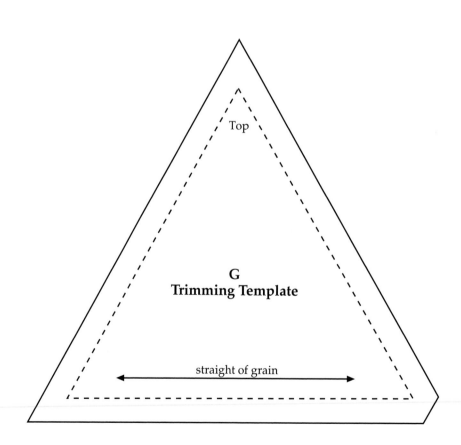

Top

**G
Trimming Template**

straight of grain

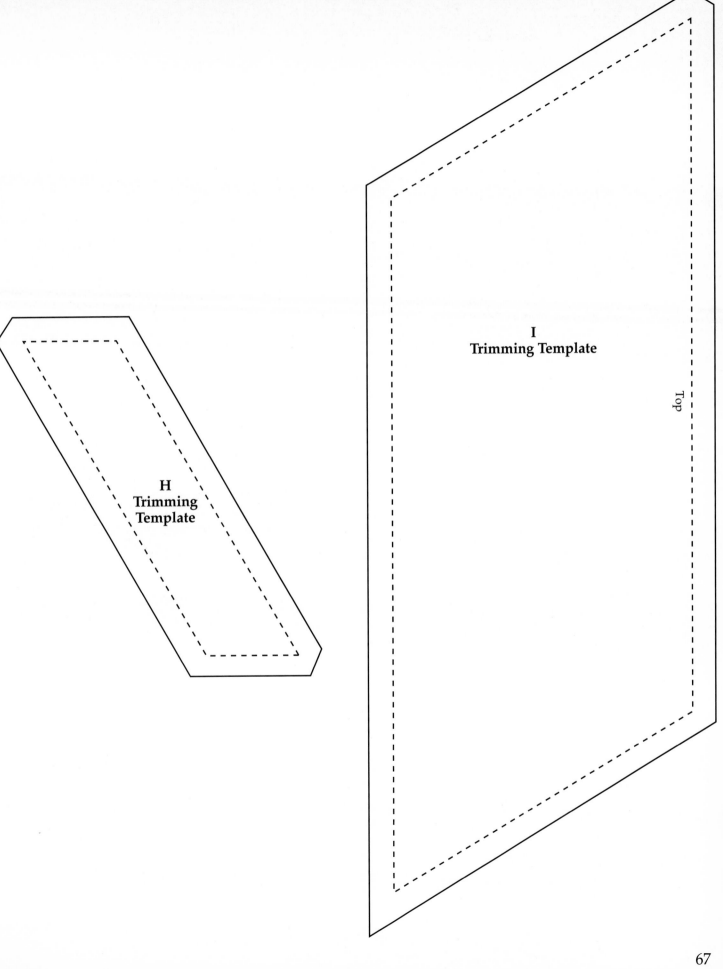

H
Trimming
Template

I
Trimming Template

Top

SCRAPPY GEESE QUILT

We eliminated the tiny triangles traditionally used in making Flying Geese blocks, opting for a faster and easier technique to create our Geese and Square-in-a-Square units. Simply stitch small squares onto rectangles or larger squares and trim them along the diagonal seams for quick, accurate points.

Finished Quilt Size: 75¹/₂" x 105¹/₂"
Finished Block Size: 12" x 12"

BEFORE YOU BEGIN

*We recommend that you read the entire **Quick-Method ABC's** (pg. 4) before beginning this project to become familiar with rotary cutting and speed-piecing techniques. This project especially emphasizes the following skills:*

Making Geese Units (pg. 29)
Making Square-in-a-Square Units (pg. 30)

YARDAGE

Yardage is based on 45"w fabric.

- ¹/₄ yd *each* of 16 assorted prints
- 9³/₄ yds of white solid
- 1¹/₂ yds of red print
  7 yds for backing
  1 yd for binding
  120" x 120" batting

CUTTING

All cutting measurements include seam allowances.

1. **From *each* assorted print:**
   - Cut 3 strips 2"w. From these strips, cut 24 **rectangles** 2" x 3¹/₂".

2. **From white solid:**
   - Cut 20 strips 3¹/₂"w. From these strips, cut 58 **sashing strips** 3¹/₂" x 12¹/₂".
   - Cut 2 strips 3¹/₂"w. From these strips, cut 16 **medium squares** 3¹/₂" x 3¹/₂".
   - Cut 4 strips 6¹/₂"w. From these strips, cut 24 **large squares** 6¹/₂" x 6¹/₂".
   - Cut 65 strips 2"w. From these strips, cut 1,292 **small squares** 2" x 2".
   - Cut 2 lengthwise strips 6¹/₂" x 93¹/₂" for **side borders**.
   - Cut 2 lengthwise strips 6¹/₂" x 63¹/₂" for **top/bottom borders**.

3. **From red print:**
   - Cut 1 strip 6¹/₂"w. From this strip, cut 4 **large squares** 6¹/₂" x 6¹/₂".
   - Cut 12 strips 3¹/₂"w. From these strips, cut 131 **small squares** 3¹/₂" x 3¹/₂".

PIECING

1. Using 1 print **rectangle** and 2 white **small squares,** follow Steps 1 - 5 of **Making Geese Units**, pg. 29, to make **Geese Unit**. Make 384 **Geese Units**.

Geese Unit (make 384)

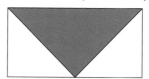

2. Sew 4 different **Geese Units** together to make **Unit 1**. Using the same color combination, make a total of 24 **Unit 1's**.

Unit 1 (make 24)

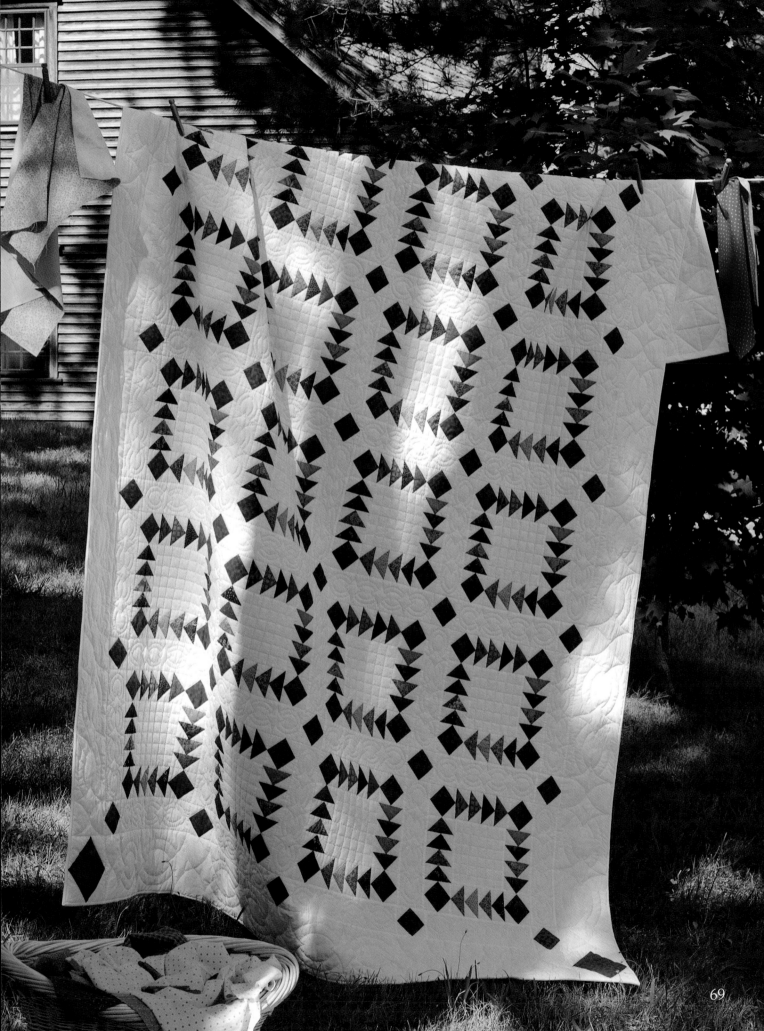

3. Repeat Step 2 to make 24 **Unit 2's**, 24 **Unit 3's**, and 24 **Unit 4's**.

Unit 2 (make 24)

Unit 3 (make 24)

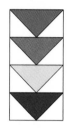

Unit 4 (make 24)

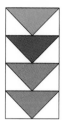

4. Using 4 white **small squares** and 1 red **small square**, follow Steps 1 - 5 of **Making Square-in-a-Square Units**, pg. 30, to make **Unit 5**. Make 131 **Unit 5's**.

Unit 5 (make 131)

5. Using 4 white **medium squares** and 1 red **large square**, repeat Step 4 to make **Unit 6**. Make 4 **Unit 6's**.

Unit 6 (make 4)

6. Sew 2 **Unit 5's** and 1 **Unit 1** together to make **Unit 7**. Make 24 **Unit 7's**.

Unit 7 (make 24)

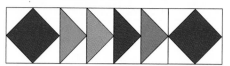

7. Sew 1 **Unit 2**, 1 **Unit 3**, and 1 white **large square** together to make **Unit 8**. Make 24 **Unit 8's**.

Unit 8 (make 24)

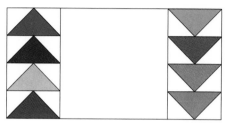

8. Sew 2 **Unit 5's** and 1 **Unit 4** together to make **Unit 9**. Make 24 **Unit 9's**.

Unit 9 (make 24)

9. Sew 1 each of **Unit 7**, **Unit 8**, and **Unit 9** together to make **Scrappy Geese Block**. Make 24 **Scrappy Geese Blocks**.

Scrappy Geese Block (make 24)

10. Sew 5 **sashing strips** and 4 **Scrappy Geese Blocks** together to make **Row A**. Make 6 **Row A's**.

Row A (make 6)

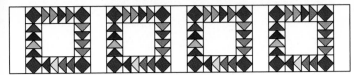

11. Sew 5 **Unit 5's** and 4 **sashing strips** together to make **Row B**. Make 7 **Row B's**.

Row B (make 7)

12. Refer to **Quilt Top Diagram** to sew **Rows** together to complete center design area of quilt top.
13. Sew 1 **Unit 6** to each end of **top** and **bottom borders**. Sew **side**, then **top** and **bottom borders** to center design area to complete quilt top.

FINISHING

1. Follow **Quilting**, pg. 32, to mark, layer, and quilt using **Quilting Diagram** as a suggestion. **Large** and **Small Diamond Chain** quilting patterns are on pg. 92.
2. Cut a 32" square of binding fabric. Follow **Binding**, pg. 35, to bind quilt using 2¼"w bias binding with mitered corners.

Quilting Diagram

Quilt Top Diagram

71

FLOWER BASKET WALL HANGING

Create a basket of beautiful blooms using floral print fabrics and a few handy tips for working with templates and set-in seams! Set together without sashing strips, the vivid baskets stand out beautifully against the lighter background. The wall hanging is accented with a contrasting inner border and binding.

Finished Wall Hanging Size: 33½" x 33½"
Finished Block Size: 9" x 9"

BEFORE YOU BEGIN

*We recommend that you read the entire **Quick-Method ABC's** (pg. 4) before beginning this project to become familiar with rotary cutting and speed-piecing techniques. This project especially emphasizes the following skills:*

> *Cutting Diamonds (pg. 17)*
> *Working with Diamonds and Set-in Seams (pg. 23)*
> *Adding Mitered Borders (pg. 25)*

YARDAGE

Yardage is based on 45"w fabric.

- ½ yd of burgundy print
- ¼ yd of burgundy solid
- 1¾ yds of tan print
- ¼ yd of dark green print
- ¼ yd of green print
  1¼ yds for backing
  ¼ yd for hanging sleeve
  ½ yd for binding
  38" x 38" batting

You will also need:
> tracing paper or template plastic

CUTTING

All cutting measurements include seam allowances.

1. **From burgundy print:**
   - Cut 4 strips 1¼"w for **inner borders**.
   - Cut 1 strip 2⅜"w. Refer to **Cutting Diamonds**, pg. 17, to cut 10 **diamonds** at a 45° angle with a finished height of 1⅞".

2. **From burgundy solid:**
   - Cut 1 strip 2⅜"w. Refer to **Cutting Diamonds**, pg. 17, to cut 10 **diamonds** at a 45° angle with a finished height of 1⅞".

3. **From tan print:**
   - Cut 4 strips 3½"w for **outer borders**.
   - Cut 1 strip 14"w. From this strip, cut 1 square 14" x 14". Cut square twice diagonally to make 4 quarter-square triangles for **setting triangles**.
   - Cut 1 strip 7¼"w. From this strip, cut 2 squares 7¼" x 7¼". Cut squares once diagonally to make 4 half-square triangles for **corner triangles**.
   - Cut 2 strips 3⅛"w. From these strips, cut 5 **squares** 3⅛" x 3⅛" and 10 **rectangles** 3⅛" x 4¼".
   - Cut 1 strip 5"w. From this strip, cut 3 squares 5" x 5". Cut squares twice diagonally to make 12 **quarter-square triangles**. (You will need 10 and have 2 left over.)
   - Cut 1 strip 6⅛"w. From this strip, cut 3 squares 6⅛" x 6⅛". Cut squares once diagonally to make 6 **half-square triangles**. (You will need 5 and have 1 left over.)

4. **From dark green print:**
   - Cut 1 strip 4⅝"w. From this strip, cut 3 squares 4⅝" x 4⅝". Cut squares once diagonally to make 6 half-square triangles for **large triangles**. (You will need 5 and have 1 left over.)

5. **From green print:**
   - Cut 1 strip 3½"w. From this strip, cut 5 squares 3½" x 3½". Cut squares once diagonally to make 10 half-square triangles for **small triangles**.

PIECING

1. Using marking template patterns, pg. 77, follow **Using Marking Templates**, pg. 23, to mark **squares**, **small triangles**, and **diamonds**.
2. (*Note:* For Steps 2 - 4, follow **Working with Diamonds and Set-in Seams**, pg. 23, to sew pieces together.) Sew 1 burgundy print and 1 burgundy solid **diamond** together to make **Unit 1**. Make 10 **Unit 1's**.

Unit 1 (make 10)

3. Sew 2 **Unit 1's** together to make **Unit 2**. Make 5 **Unit 2's**.

Unit 2 (make 5)

4. Sew 1 **Unit 2**, 2 **quarter-square triangles**, and 1 **square** together to make **Unit 3**. Make 5 **Unit 3's**.

Unit 3 (make 5)

5. Sew 1 **large triangle** and 1 **Unit 3** together to make **Unit 4**. Make 5 **Unit 4's**.

Unit 4 (make 5)

6. Sew 1 **rectangle** and 1 **small triangle** together to make **Unit 5**. Make 5 **Unit 5's**.

Unit 5 (make 5)

7. Sew 1 **small triangle** and 1 **rectangle** together to make **Unit 6**. Make 5 **Unit 6's**.

Unit 6 (make 5)

8. Sew 1 **Unit 5**, 1 **Unit 6**, and 1 **Unit 4** together to make **Unit 7**. Make 5 **Unit 7's**.

Unit 7 (make 5)

9. Sew 1 **half-square triangle** and 1 **Unit 7** together to make **Flower Basket Block**. Make 5 **Flower Basket Blocks**.

Flower Basket Block (make 5)

10. Referring to **Assembly Diagram**, sew **corner triangles**, **setting triangles**, and **Flower Basket Blocks** together in diagonal rows. Sew rows together to complete center design area of wall hanging top.

11. Sew 1 **inner border** and 1 **outer border** together to make **Border Unit**. Make 4 **Border Units**.

Border Unit (make 4)

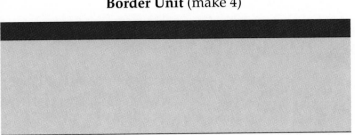

12. Referring to **Wall Hanging Top Diagram**, pg. 76, follow **Adding Mitered Borders**, pg. 25, to sew **Border Units** to center design area to complete wall hanging top.

FINISHING

1. Follow **Quilting**, pg. 32, to mark, layer, and quilt using **Quilting Diagram** as a suggestion. **Large** and **Small Basketweave** quilting patterns are on pg. 93.

2. Follow **Making a Hanging Sleeve**, pg. 37, to make a hanging sleeve.

3. Follow **Binding**, pg. 35, to bind wall hanging using 2¹/₄"w straight-grain binding with overlapped corners.

Assembly Diagram

Quilting Diagram

Wall Hanging Top Diagram

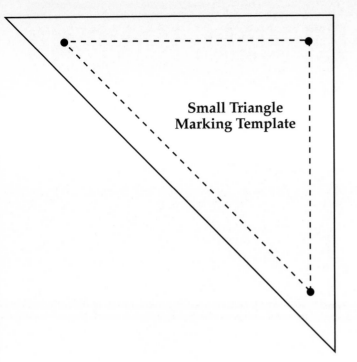

**Small Triangle
Marking Template**

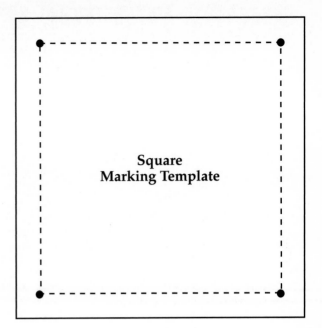

**Square
Marking Template**

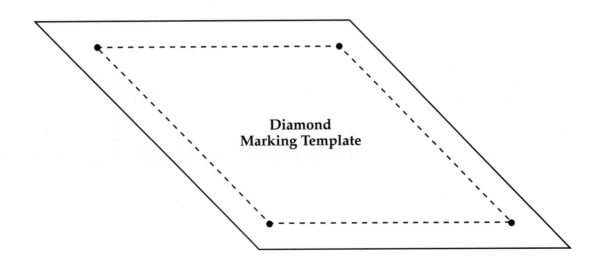

**Diamond
Marking Template**

SHOOT FOR THE STARS WALL HANGING

Golden eight-pointed stars glisten against the midnight hues of this wall hanging. The celestial motifs appear when pieced triangle and rectangle units are alternated with large plain squares in diagonal rows. For added interest, partial stars are pieced into the wide border.

Finished Wall Hanging Size: 32" x 40"

BEFORE YOU BEGIN

*We recommend that you read the entire **Quick-Method ABC's** (pg. 4) before beginning this project to become familiar with rotary cutting and speed-piecing techniques. This project especially emphasizes the following skills:*

> *Cutting Equilateral Triangles (pg. 16)*
> *Cutting Half Rectangles (pg. 20)*
> *Using Trimming Templates (pg. 21)*

YARDAGE

Yardage is based on 45"w fabric.

- ¾ yd of gold print
- 1 yd of medium blue print
- 1⅛ yds of dark blue print
  1½ yds for backing
  ¼ yd for hanging sleeve
  ¾ yd for binding
  36" x 44" batting

You will also need:
> tracing paper or template plastic

CUTTING

All cutting measurements include seam allowances.

1. **From gold print:**
   - Cut 1 strip 3¾"w. From this strip, cut 7 squares 3¾" x 3¾". Cut squares twice diagonally to make 28 **quarter-square triangles**.
   - Cut 1 strip 2¼"w. From this strip, cut 17 **squares** 2¼" x 2¼".

- Cut 4 strips 2¹¹/₁₆"w. From these strips, cut 96 rectangles 2¹¹/₁₆" x 1⁹/₁₆". Leaving rectangles stacked in pairs with wrong sides together, cut each pair of rectangles once diagonally to make 96 **half rectangles** and 96 **reverse half rectangles**.

rectangle (cut 96)

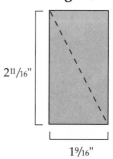

2¹¹/₁₆"

1⁹/₁₆"

half rectangle (cut 96)

reverse half rectangle (cut 96)

2. **From medium blue print:**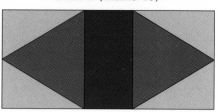
   - Cut 4 strips 2¼"w. Use these strips and refer to **Cutting Equilateral Triangles**, pg. 16, to cut 96 **equilateral triangles** with a finished height of 1½".
   - Cut 1 strip 3⅝"w. From this strip, cut 2 squares 3⅝" x 3⅝". Cut squares once diagonally to make 4 half-square triangles for **corner setting triangles**.
   - Cut 1 strip 6¾"w. From this strip, cut 3 squares 6¾" x 6¾". Cut squares twice diagonally to make 12 quarter-square triangles for **setting triangles**. (You will need 10 and have 2 left over.)
   - Cut 1 strip 4⅜"w. From this strip, cut 6 **squares** 4⅜" x 4⅜".

3. **From dark blue print:** ▪
   - Cut 2 strips 3" x 40" for **side outer borders**.
   - Cut 2 strips 3" x 27" for **top/bottom outer borders**.
   - Cut 2 strips 2¼"w. From these strips, cut 48 **rectangle A's** 2¼" x 1⅜".
   - Cut 3 strips 1¾". From these cut 10 **rectangle B's** 1¾" x 6", 4 **rectangle C's** 1¾" x 3¼", and 4 **rectangle D's** 1¾" x 4½".
   - Cut 1 strip 2⅛"w. From this strip, cut 14 squares 2⅛" x 2⅛". Cut squares once diagonally to make 28 **half-square triangles**.
   - Cut 2 strips 4⅜"w. From these strips, cut 12 **squares** 4⅜" x 4⅜".

PIECING

1. Use patterns, pg. 82, and follow **Using Trimming Templates**, pg. 21, to make trimming templates for half rectangle and reverse half rectangle. Trim 96 **half rectangles** and 96 **reverse half rectangles**.
2. Sew 1 **half rectangle**, 1 **equilateral triangle**, and 1 **reverse half rectangle** together to make **Unit 1**. Make 96 **Unit 1's**.

Unit 1 (make 96)

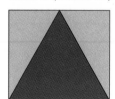

3. Sew 2 **Unit 1's** and 1 dark blue **rectangle A** together to make **Unit 2**. Make 48 **Unit 2's**.

Unit 2 (make 48)

4. Referring to **Assembly Diagram**, sew gold **quarter-square triangles**, **corner setting triangles**, **setting triangles**, **Unit 2's**, dark blue **squares**, medium blue **squares**, and gold **squares** into rows.
5. Sew rows together to complete center design area of wall hanging top.
6. Sew 2 dark blue **half-square triangles** and 1 gold **quarter-square triangle** together to make **Unit 3**. Make 14 **Unit 3's**.

Unit 3 (make 14)

7. Sew 2 dark blue **rectangle C's**, 2 dark blue **rectangle B's**, and 3 **Unit 3's** together to make **Top Inner Border**. Repeat for **Bottom Inner Border**.

Top/Bottom Inner Border (make 2)

8. Sew 2 dark blue **rectangle D's**, 3 dark blue **rectangle B's**, and 4 **Unit 3's** together to make **Side Inner Border**. Make 2 **Side Inner Borders**.

Side Inner Border (make 2)

9. Referring to **Wall Hanging Top Diagram**, pg. 82, sew **Top**, **Bottom**, then **Side Inner Borders** to center design area. Repeat to add **outer borders** to complete wall hanging top.

FINISHING

1. Follow **Quilting**, pg. 32, to mark, layer, and quilt using **Quilting Diagram**, pg. 82, as a suggestion. **Circle of Stars** and **Star** quilting patterns are on pg. 94.
2. Follow **Making a Hanging Sleeve**, pg. 37, to make a hanging sleeve.
3. Cut a 22" square of binding fabric. Follow **Binding**, pg. 35, to bind wall hanging using 2¼"w bias binding with mitered corners.

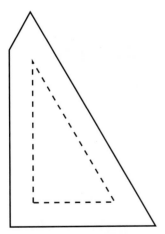

**Half Rectangle
Trimming Template**

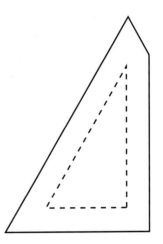

**Reverse Half Rectangle
Trimming Template**

PILLOW PRIMER

When you want to practice the quick methods you've just learned, but don't have time for a full-size quilt, try one of these pleasing pillows! Just the right size for a weekend project, our Pinwheel, Ohio Star, and Schoolhouse designs are pieced using the best of our time-saving tips.

PINWHEEL PILLOW

Finished Pillow Size: 12" x 12" (including ruffle)

BEFORE YOU BEGIN
*We recommend that you read the entire **Quick-Method ABC's** (pg. 4) before beginning this project to become familiar with rotary cutting and speed-piecing techniques.*

YARDAGE
Yardage is based on 45"w fabric.

- ▓ ½ yd of red print
- ☐ ¼ yd of white solid
- ■ ⅛ yd of blue print
  13" x 13" pillow top backing
  8½" x 8½" pillow back
  13" x 13" batting

You will also need:
polyester fiberfill

CUTTING
All cutting measurements include seam allowances.

1. **From red print:** ▓
   - Cut 1 strip 2⅞"w. From this strip, cut 2 squares 2⅞" x 2⅞". Cut squares once diagonally to make 4 **half-square triangles**.
   - Cut 2 strips 5"w for **ruffle**.

2. **From white solid:** ☐
   - Cut 1 strip 2⅞"w. From this strip, cut 2 squares 2⅞" x 2⅞". Cut squares once diagonally to make 4 **half-square triangles**.
   - Cut 1 strip 2½"w. From this strip, cut 4 **rectangles** 2½" x 4½".

3. **From blue print:** ■
   - Cut 1 strip 2½"w. From this strip, cut 4 **squares** 2½" x 2½".

PIECING

1. Place 1 red **half-square triangle** and 1 white **half-square triangle** right sides together. Sew triangles together along the long edge (**Fig. 1**). Press seam allowance toward the red fabric to make **Unit 1**. Make 4 **Unit 1's**.

Fig. 1   **Unit 1** (make 4)

2. Sew 2 **Unit 1's** together to make **Unit 2**. Make 2 **Unit 2's**.

Unit 2 (make 2)

3. Sew **Unit 2's** together to make **Pinwheel Unit**.

Pinwheel Unit (make 1)

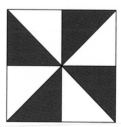

4. Sew 2 **rectangles** and **Pinwheel Unit** together to make **Unit 3**.

Unit 3 (make 1)

5. Sew 1 **rectangle** and 2 **squares** together to make **Unit 4**. Make 2 **Unit 4's**.

Unit 4 (make 2)

6. Sew **Unit 3** and **Unit 4's** together to complete Pinwheel Block for **Pillow Top**.

Pillow Top

PILLOW FINISHING

1. Follow **Quilting**, pg. 32, to mark, layer, and quilt in the ditch along seamlines. Trim batting and backing even with pillow top.
2. Matching right sides, use a $1/4$" seam allowance to sew short edges of **ruffle** strips together to form a large circle; press seam allowances open. With wrong sides together and matching raw edges, fold ruffle in half; press.
3. To gather ruffle, place quilting thread $3/16$" from raw edge of ruffle. Using a medium width zigzag stitch with medium stitch length, stitch over quilting thread, being careful not to catch quilting thread in stitching. Pull quilting thread, drawing up gathers to fit pillow top.
4. Matching raw edges, baste ruffle to right side of pillow top.
5. Place pillow back and pillow top right sides together. Using a $1/4$" seam allowance, sew pillow top and back together, leaving an opening at bottom edge for turning.
6. Turn pillow right side out, carefully pushing corners outward. Stuff with polyester fiberfill and sew opening closed by hand.

OHIO STAR PILLOW

Finished Pillow Size: 10" x 10"

BEFORE YOU BEGIN

*We recommend that you read the entire **Quick-Method ABC's** (pg. 4) before beginning this project to become familiar with rotary cutting and speed-piecing techniques.*

YARDAGE

Yardage is based on 45"w fabric.

- ◼ $1/3$ yd of blue print
- ☐ $1/3$ yd of white solid
- ◼ $1/3$ yd of red print
  14" x 14" pillow top backing
  $9^{1}/_{2}$" x $9^{1}/_{2}$" pillow back
  14" x 14" batting

You will also need:
  polyester fiberfill

CUTTING

All cutting measurements include seam allowances.

1. **From blue print:**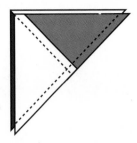
   - Cut 1 strip 3½"w. From this strip, cut 1 **square** 3½" x 3½".
   - Cut 1 strip 4¼"w. From this strip, cut 2 squares 4¼" x 4¼". Cut squares twice diagonally to make 8 **quarter-square triangles**.

2. **From white solid:**
   - Cut 1 strip 3½"w. From this strip, cut 4 **squares** 3½" x 3½".
   - Cut 1 strip 4¼"w. From this strip, cut 2 squares 4¼" x 4¼". Cut squares twice diagonally to make 8 **quarter-square triangles**.

3. **From red print:**
   - Cut 2 **strips** 2¼"w for binding.

PIECING

1. Place 1 blue and 1 white **quarter-square triangle** right sides together. Sew triangles together along 1 short side (**Fig. 1**). Press seam allowance toward the blue fabric to make **Unit 1**. Make 8 **Unit 1's**.

Fig. 1

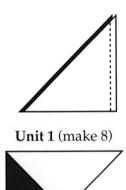

Unit 1 (make 8)

2. Place 2 **Unit 1's** right sides together and matching seams. Sew together along long edges to make **Unit 2** (**Fig. 2**). Make 4 **Unit 2's**.

Fig. 2

Unit 2 (make 4)

3. Sew **Unit 2's**, white **squares**, and blue **square** together to make Ohio Star Block for **Pillow Top**.

Pillow Top

![Ohio Star Block diagram]

PILLOW FINISHING

1. Follow **Quilting**, pg. 32, to mark, layer, and quilt using **Quilting Diagram**, pg. 50, as a suggestion.
2. Trim batting and backing even with pillow top. Place pillow top and pillow back wrong sides together; sew together using a ¼" seam allowance, leaving an opening for stuffing. Stuff pillow with fiberfill and sew opening closed.
3. For binding, sew **strips** together along 1 short edge; press seam allowance open. Matching wrong sides and raw edges, press strip in half lengthwise.
4. Follow **Attaching Binding with Mitered Corners**, pg. 36, to bind edges of pillow.

SCHOOLHOUSE PILLOW

Finished Pillow Size: 15½" x 15½"

BEFORE YOU BEGIN

*We recommend that you read the entire **Quick-Method ABC's** (pg. 4) before beginning this project to become familiar with rotary cutting and speed-piecing techniques.*

We made this pillow top by adding borders to the Schoolhouse Block from the Schoolhouse Wall Hanging. Please refer to the wall hanging instructions (pg. 58) when making pillow top.

YARDAGE

Yardage is based on 45"w fabric.

- ☐ 1 yd of white solid
- ■ 1 yd of blue print
- ■ ¼ yd of red print
  19" x 19" pillow top backing
  16" x 16" pillow back
  2 yds of ¼" cord for welting
  19" x 19" batting

You will also need:
   polyester fiberfill

CUTTING

All cutting measurements include seam allowances. Label pieces for easy identification.

1. **From white solid:** ☐
   - Follow Step 1 of **Cutting** for **Schoolhouse Wall Hanging**, pg. 58, to cut the following:
     2 **B's**
     1 **D**
     1 **E**
     1 **F**
     1 **Reverse F**
     1 **H**
     1 **K**
     2 **O's**
     1 **R**
     1 **T**
   - Cut 2 strips 1½" x 19" for **top** and **bottom outer borders**. Cut 2 strips 1½" x 17" for **side outer borders**.
   - Piecing as necessary, cut a 2 yd (72") length of 2¼"w bias strip for welting.

2. **From blue print:** ■
   - Follow Step 2 of **Cutting** for **Schoolhouse Wall Hanging**, pg. 60, to cut the following:
     1 **A**
     1 **C**
     1 **G**
     1 **I**
     1 **J**
     2 **L's**
     1 **M**
     1 **N**
     2 **P's**
     1 **Q**
     1 **S**

3. **From red print:** ■
   - Cut 2 strips 1" x 16" for **side inner borders**. Cut 2 strips 1" x 17" for **top** and **bottom inner borders**.

PIECING

1. Follow Steps 1 - 11 of **Piecing** for **Schoolhouse Wall Hanging**, pg. 61, to make **Schoolhouse Block**.

Schoolhouse Block

2. Sew **side**, then **top** and **bottom inner borders** to **Schoolhouse Block**. Repeat to add **outer borders** to complete **Pillow Top**.

Pillow Top

PILLOW FINISHING

1. Follow **Quilting**, pg. 32, to mark, layer, and quilt using **Quilting Diagram**, pg. 65, as a suggestion. Trim batting and backing even with pillow top.
2. To make welting, lay cord along center of bias **strip** on wrong side of fabric; fold strip over cord. Using a zipper foot, machine baste along length of strip close to cord. Trim seam allowance to 1/4".
3. Matching raw edges and beginning and ending 3" from ends of welting, baste welting to right side of pillow top. To make turning corners easier, clip seam allowance of welting at corners.

4. Remove approximately 3" of seam stitching at 1 end of welting; fold fabric away from cord. Trim remaining end of welting so that cord ends meet exactly. Fold short edge of welting fabric 1/2" to wrong side; fold fabric back over area where ends meet (**Fig. 1**). Baste remainder of welting to pillow top close to cord.

Fig. 1

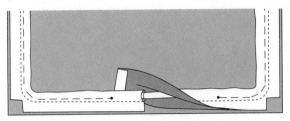

5. Place pillow back and pillow top right sides together. Stitching as close as possible to the welting, sew pillow top and back together, leaving an opening at bottom edge for turning.
6. Turn pillow right side out, carefully pushing corners outward. Stuff with polyester fiberfill and sew opening closed by hand.

QUILTING PATTERNS

Heart Wreath

Clamshell

Petal

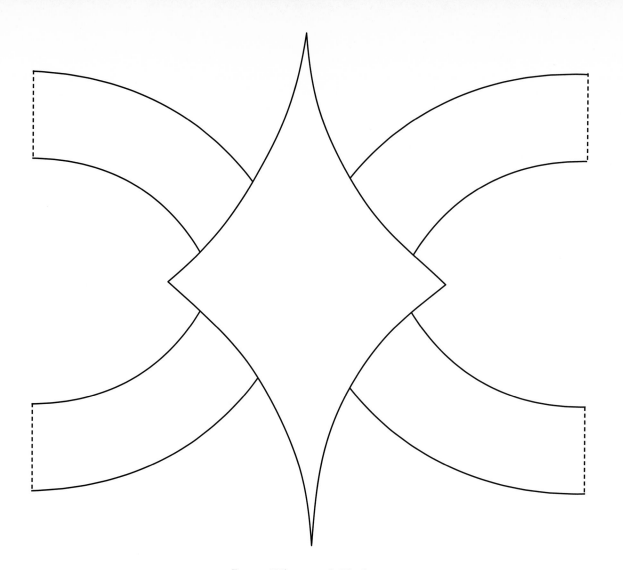

Large Diamond Chain

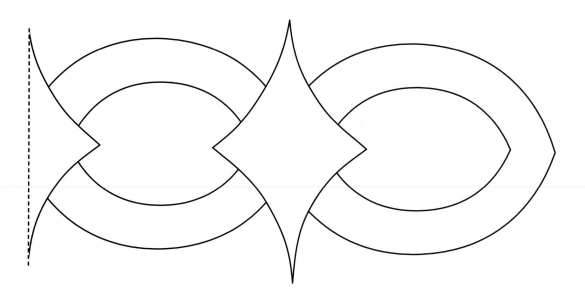

Small Diamond Chain

92

Large Basketweave

Small Basketweave

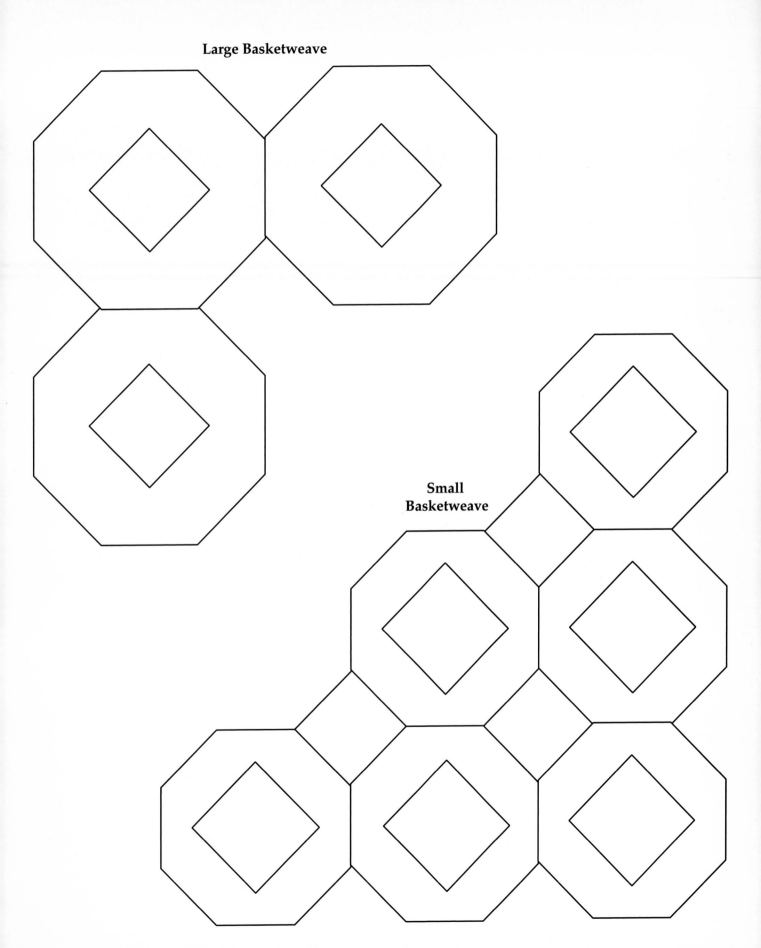

Circle of Stars

Star

INDEX

CREDITS

We want to extend a warm *thank you* to the generous people who allowed us to photograph our projects at their homes: Carl and Monte Brunck and Nancy and Duncan Porter.

Thanks also go to Viking Husqvarna Sewing Machine Company of Cleveland, Ohio, for providing the sewing machines used to make many of the projects in this book.

To Magna IV Color Imaging of Little Rock, Arkansas, we say thank you for the superb color reproduction and excellent pre-press preparation.

We especially want to thank photographers Mark Mathews, Larry Pennington, Karen Shirey, and Ken West of Peerless Photography, Little Rock, Arkansas, and Jerry R. Davis of Jerry Davis Photography, Little Rock, Arkansas, for their time, patience, and excellent work.

We extend a sincere *thank you* to all the people who assisted in making and testing the projects in this book: Margie Berry, Valerie Doiel, Wanda Fite, Patricia Galas, Betty Gill, Grace Grame, Ethel Jacobson, Liz Lane, Barbara Middleton, Helen Rowe, Ruby Solida, Glenda Taylor, and the quilters of the Mayflower Senior Citizens Center: Myrtle Aycock, Elois McCaghren, Fay McCoy, and Elsie Teas.